THE
OPINIONATED
PALATE

THE OPINIONATED PALATE

*Passions and Peeves
on Eating and Food*

BARBARA KAFKA

WILLIAM MORROW AND COMPANY, INC.
NEW YORK

It is the policy of William Morrow and Company Inc., and its imprints and affiliates, recognizing the importance of preserving what has been written, to print the books we publish on acid-free paper, and we exert our best efforts to that end.

Library of Congress Cataloging-in-Publication Data

Kafka, Barbara.
   The opinionated palate : passions and peeves on eating and food / Barbara Kafka.
      p.   cm.
   Includes index.
   ISBN 0-688-09982-3
   1. Food.   2. Cookery.   3. Gastronomy.   I. Title.
TX355.5.K24   1992   91-28646
641—dc20   CIP

Printed in the United States of America

First Edition

1 2 3 4 5 6 7 8 9 10

BOOK DESIGN BY NICOLA MAZZELLA

For Ernie

ACKNOWLEDGMENTS

MORE THAN MOST books, *The Opinionated Palate* owes its very being to editors and publishers as most of the material in it was originally published in some form in magazines or newspapers, which indicates my inability to write without the coercion of a deadline and the carrot of potential payment.

But articles must be formed into a book. A book of essays may not be the most apparently commercial of ventures, so it is with special warmth than I thank my editor and friend of many years at William Morrow, Ann Bramson. Without her, there would be fewer and less good books. I thank Al Marchioni, the publisher, who has tried to ease my creative and financial path and succeeded. Lisa Queen, the subrights director, who represents me to the world, is one of the best friends a writer could have. Laurie Orseck, the line editor on this book, has provided the objective eye that is especially needed when a writer attempts to weld disparate pieces into a whole.

As always, I thank Leo Lerman who, from my earliest days at *Mademoiselle,* has guided me—especially toward writing about food—and helped me and who for several years, as the feature editor of *Vogue,* bought pieces from me and helped to shape them.

I thank Alexander Liberman, who first thought it was time for me to return to *Vogue* after my hesitant start many years earlier under Allene Talmey, and Amy Gross, who took over from Leo both the job and the intelligent support for my monthly stint.

When the time came for me to separate from *Vogue,* my work was adopted by Jane Montand, then editor of *Gourmet,* and subsequently by Gail Zweigenthal, the current editor. They gave me the opportunity to have a monthly page in which to write as I wished about the many facets of the world of food. That column is called *An Opinionated Palate.* Condé Nast, the home of all these magazines, has graciously given me permission to use this title for my book, although all the material does not come from the pages of *Gourmet.*

The New York Times has been another haven for my work, The Living Section, *The New York Times Magazine* and the Entertainment Section of *The New York Times Magazine*. I have been fortunate in having intelligent and amusing editors there as well: Margo Slade, Angela Dotson and Eric Asimov, Penelope Green and Linda Wells, and Alison McFarland and Anne de Ravel.

Food & Wine, with its editors Ila Stanger, Carol Lally, Warren Picower and Malachy Duffy, has provided me the opportunity to write on some topics I particularly enjoy.

Family Circle and its editors, Jackie Leo and Jean Hewitt, have been a regular and informative part of my working world for several years.

The Radcliffe Quarterly and its editor, Ada Press, have been splendid extensions of my alma mater and have let me chew on a broad range of thoughts.

In my own office, it has been possible to work because others have competently undertaken a wide variety of chores—cheerfully—freeing me to write: Esti Marpet, Sydney Watts and Nancy Messing, during the compiling of this book, although over the years there is a much longer list of those who made my work easier. While this is not a recipe book, during its writing I have been regularly involved in the development and writing of recipes, and it is because at various times the following extremely able people have been helping

9

me that I could turn my mind to more discursive prose: Lee Ann Cox, Anna Brandenburger and Christopher Styler.

Food and cooking is such a vast subject that one can hardly perceive, let alone define, the nature of the contributions that others have made. I have relied on Corby Kummer for fertilizing conversation and James Beard for erudition and a certain measure of constructive abrasion as well as warm support.

CONTENTS

FOREWORD

RUSSELL LYNES ONCE wrote the charming *Book of Snobs*. In it, he pointed out that the worst snobs are those, like himself, who think they can define what a snob is. I find myself in much the same position with this book of opinions. Opinions always imply standards. Who decides what is good, pleasant, attractive, even virtuous or the converse and by what standard? For better or worse, in this book: "Who sez?" I sez; that's who.

Many of the standards are based on personal opinion derived from my own tastes and pleasures and a consensus based on historical and international values. Ripe fruit is better than fruit without perfume or flavor. The limitations to this approach are those of my personal experience—if I haven't tasted or experienced something, I cannot share it with you—and of my judgments. If you like bland food without texture, you are going to hate most of my opinions except when it comes to mashed potatoes.

So, you need to know something about me to understand my tastes and see if they make sense to you. I am urban and American; but I love to garden in the relatively unforgiving climate of Vermont. I travel mainly in Europe and the Americas. My knowledge of Asian cooking comes from passionate eating and endless reading as well as lots of looking at things in museums rather than from first-hand experience.

I know that my tastes and experiences are very American, but that neither means native American nor rock-ribbed Anglo-Saxon. I firmly believe that if you have landed here and live here, you are American no matter what your ethnic background. If you cook the foods of your background or use its culinary ingredients, you can call it American. What's more, your cuisine has probably added a great deal to a wide variety of kinds of cooking.

I find food to be a fascinating subject. Its style, its history, its flavors, its production permit one to learn something about sociology, anthropology, economics, agriculture, art, history, architecture and an unending list of other fields. Food, the need to acquire it, our pleasure in it and the rites we build around it are the things that bind all human beings together. It provides not only great delight but also the delight, if a frustrating one, of endless learning. No one can know all about it.

The essays in this book have been written over several years and echo my thoughts and interests at various times. Although in rereading them I find that my point of view has remained fairly stable, you may come across divergent attitudes . . . no more divergent than what I may want for dinner on one night rather than on another. Where I have treated a subject that pleases me, such as salad, more than once, I have combined the pieces to make a whole since I don't think that my work is so valuable or of such historic interest that these changes are destructive.

I only hope that you will find an idea or turn of phrase that pleases you, an emotion that you share or get a laugh now and then.

THE ART AND CRAFT OF FOOD WRITING

YOUR DAUGHTER DOES WHAT?

FOR MANY YEARS now, the answer has been, "She writes about food." It was certainly the bane of my mother's existence that my semitriumphant graduation from Radcliffe did not lead to law school—she herself is a lawyer—politics or some other public-spirited career. If I insisted on the somewhat formless life of a writer, why could I not at least write major novels or disquisitions on serious subjects? I have asked myself the same questions many times over the passing years. The answer has always been that I can't.

My mother, I think, has become numb, if not totally reconciled, to my life among the pots and pans.Some of the novocaine has been applied by the increasing fashionableness of food and eating. I have gone from infra dig to glamour in just over one generation. Those very friends of Mother's who in the fifties and sixties looked at her so incredulously now crave restaurant reservations and even my time to talk to their grandchildren, men included, about their wishes for a "career" in what was previously the blue-collar-world of food.

For it is true that when I started out to write about food, as much by chance as by intention, women like us cooked for ourselves when we were young; but in an urban environment, success meant that eventually somebody else would do the cooking for you. In some ways, we still observe the same pattern now that we are working women. Instead of cooks at home, we have chefs in restaurants. The old pattern placed cooks in the servant category. The way people got into the restaurant business and the way they were trained reinforced that class-oriented view.

Restaurant kitchens were largely staffed by inexpensive, uneducated labor glad to accept conditions of near-servitude for entry-level jobs in the American economy. Their superiors, the trained chefs, had usually been trained in an apprenticeship system that set them to work no later than fourteen, aborting conventional schooling. Long and hard work hours left little time and energy for self-improvement. The chefs themselves generally came from rather poor families, drawn to the arduous apprenticeship by the knowledge that, at least, they would be fed and housed.

These class distinctions were reinforced by the fact that it was not until several years after World War I that respectable women could be seen dining out at anything other than an elegant hotel dining room: "Don't put your daughter on the stage, Mrs. Worthington," could certainly have been adapted to restaurants. Women were the cooks, not chefs, only of small family-run country inns or tacky lunch counters. It was a man's world, partly due to the communal living arrangements of most apprenticeships.

There were exceptions. Fannie Farmer, Mrs. Marshall and the heirs of Mrs. Beeton all made substantial amounts of money and acquired respectable reputations writing books directed to the home audience. Much of their emphasis, however, was on running a household and on the instruction of servants. Indeed, many of the classes at the Boston Cooking School and Mrs. Marshall's were for the hired cooks. The format, then, for women in the food world was to address women like themselves rather than the professional cooks.

As time went on, more people wrote for the consumer market; but most of the field—even the elegancies of *Gourmet*—had some of the stigma of "housewife" (which "homemaker" has done very little to assuage). In the sixties, two things happened to begin to change public perception. The dropout generation had to find activities to replace the then denigrated banking, law and medicine. Food got elected "real," and Ph.D.s who couldn't find jobs in dwindling academia somehow had less feeling that they were betraying their ideals when they took jobs in restaurants. Their siblings who had returned to the land had communal kitchens, baked bread and grew things that needed to be preserved. The theme song of the era was "Alice's Restaurant." Concomitantly, French chefs were making their big move from individual obscurity as hirelings to stardom as proprietors.

The next step toward the reclamation of my good name came as more women went out to work, placing more emphasis on eating outside the home. Some of them went to work in restaurants, taking home-learned skills with them. In any case, the new generation of American chefs were people with educations, eager for invention and fame. Cooking had left the doily and the working class at the same time.

In the mid-seventies, and gathering momentum into the eighties, food was in many ways *the* social expression of the era. The desire for upward mobility resurged even as it became harder to fulfill. It was and remains a too expensive, distant, unachievable dream to upgrade the normal status symbols: home, car, children's schooling or investment status. Restaurants for the multitudes who spend most of their days away from home and share that home with much smaller or even non-existent families have become, along with the vocabulary of gastronomy, the new insignias of upward mobility and culture.

It is a culture that is easy and pleasant to learn, taught by the media. It does not require years of study and involvement. It is instant and popular, democratic in that it is available to all. It is the food writer's moment since we hold the information and trend-setting cards in the with-it sweepstakes. I still enjoy what I do; but it is ironic that having started by abandoning middle-class standards of success, I have become their avatar.

Even as the times change and more of us cook at home or search out informal, less expensive, neighborhood eating places or limit what we spend on ingredients, it is clear that we will not retreat to a time when food was not a polite subject for the dinner table. I am safe, and people seldom have to ask my mother what I do. Instead, they tell her when interviews have appeared in newspapers and magazines or I have appeared on television. Sometimes, they even read me. It seems that the only people left with questions about what I do are my mother and me.

STANDARDIZATION

IN MY VIEW, the much admired Strunk and White of *Elements of Style* fame have much that is negative for which to answer. Plain speak and standardized simple writing using untrammeled declarative sentences may communicate effectively (what an unlovely phrase!) and protect us as readers from the purple rococo; but they strip much of our reading and our lives of elegance and charm. Even in architecture, the "less is more" doctrine is under attack. I would like to attack it in writing. One has only to look at the glories of the King James edition of the Bible and compare them with the sterility of "modern" versions to see what is at risk.

This may seem like an abstruse and highfalutin' approach to food writing; but in the past food writing has often been rich and evocative, something to cherish for itself as well as for its recipes and cold information. Food, beyond the survival level, should be about pleasure, and there seems to be no reason the language in which we discuss it should not be pleasureful as well.

I am not sanctioning bombast, or sloppy metaphor. English is the exemplar of a metaphorical language. We say or write "a field of endeavor" without any conscious memory of grasses, soil or planted crops. It is only when the metaphor refuses to remain dead, as H. W. Fowler of *Modern English Usage* said—for instance, "his field of endeavor frequently took him to sea"—that the jarring context makes us realize that a metaphor has been used at all. The French really do not understand metaphor, which is one of the reasons that they still have problems with Mallarmé, who taught Metaphysical poetry and may have learned his linguistic ways from the likes of Donne. In our striving for simplicity and clarity, it would be a shame to abandon either our poetry or our linguistic inheritance.

Much in the world of food has become standardized. Some of it to clearly beneficial effect. It is good to know that our milk is sterile enough to be safe and that we are getting the vitamin D we don't get cooped up in offices away from the sun. Some of it is truly unpleasant, hideous, standardized-to-the-lowest-common-denominator packaged foods. Some of it is a two-edged sword like the standardization of recipe formats and the standardization—read popularization—of our language in mass communication.

At first glance, it seems laudable that recipes today have a rather standard format, a standard way of measuring and referring to ingredients and procedures in a fairly uniform fashion. It makes for greater professionalism. The overall level of ease in following recipes has gone up. Ingredients are listed in the order in which they are used in the recipe. We are told how much a recipe makes either in number of servings or in cups. We have become familiar with terms like "sauté" and "simmer." Many older recipes, like those in the original *Settlement Cookbook,* cannot be followed by today's less expert cooks and bakers.

And yet . . . what have we lost? The charms of personality and idiosyncrasy and, I think, even something of exactitude. When recipes are reduced to the formulaic, we are not given the texture of the culinary experience. When we are told to prepare meat for stock by melting some butter and then browning the meat, it is hardly as clear or as inviting as the following from Eliza Acton's nineteenth-century *Modern Cookery in All Its Branches:*

Rub a deep stew pan or soup-pot with butter, and lay into it three quarters of a pound of ham freed entirely from fat, skin, and rust, four pounds of leg or neck of veal, and the same weight of lean beef all cut into thick slices; set it over a clear and rather brisk fire, until the meat is of a fine amber-colour; it must be often moved, and closely watched, that it may not stick to the pan, nor burn.

Her prose makes me want to go into the kitchen and gives me a clear idea of what I should be doing and what to watch out for, all without a word of French and in one long sentence.

Even earlier, in 1623, John Knott, a chef, could write of the meat in stock: "Boil all these to Rags in Water . . . When the goodness is all boil'd out."

Of course, not all writers, even of the nineteenth century, wrote equally well. Some are evocative without being precise and others are as stodgily precise as a thirties home-ec manual without any style; but before you judge a writer, go to an early edition of his or her book. Truly successful cookbooks went through endless editions, not all of which were in the hands of the original author. Over time, many of the enticements of voice were surrendered to odd notions of progress.

Mrs. Rundell's *A New System of Domestic*

Cookery, first published anonymously in 1806, had been written up as a collection of her personal recipes for the benefit of her daughters, and found its way into print virtually unchanged via a family friend, a young publisher named John Murray, who made a fortune thereby. The book was so popular that it appeared in many editions. Some American ones sported changed titles or said they had been adapted to the American condition (false advertising). By 1847, we are up to the seventieth British edition whose title page boasts that the book is "augmented and improved . . . suited to the present state . . . of cookery" by Miss Emma Roberts—who unfortunately has improved away the directness of Mrs. Rundell's language. We are no longer in the world of "fry them to a beautiful brown."

Today, vivid writing—supposedly taboo —is confined, if it exists at all, to text and is isolated from recipes except in the books of a rare, few writers.

I suppose it would matter less if we actually gained the supposed precision; but it is often like playing bridge without having the conventions announced before the game. Authors, publishers and writers assume in common, for instance, that if an ingredient is written as one cup of strawberries, puréed, we are measuring whole berries rather than the puréed berries as in one cup puréed strawberries. Even if we remember this convention, if we follow the first instruction for measuring whole berries, having abandoned scales to our English and Continental coevals, we risk using very different amounts, as the quantity of berries in a cup or even a pint will vary vastly with the size of the berries.

As keep it short, keep it simple and generally comprehensible and keep practical have become the hallmarks of our attitude, we have also abandoned fantasy, literary reference, apposite quotation—the sport of centuries—and even when we stick to English, since it is presumed that no one has Latin, "less Greek," or even French today, we are condemned to avoiding abstruse words, to the impoverishment of our reading, like readers of children's books that, unlike *Treasure Island,* are composed in common-denominator words. We subside into the miasma of ugly technical words like "yield" and "garnish."

This means that it is the brave culinary writer indeed, often one who eschews the possibility of large sales let alone publication, who indulges in philosophy or pretends to artfulness. We are losing the possibility of more Brillat-Savarins, M.F.K. Fishers and Samuel Chamberlains.

The service piece and the unadorned recipe have their place; but if we are to have culinary literature, it is the readers who must defend, encourage and reward good writing as you find it.

KNEE HIGH TO A CUTTING BOARD

IT WAS IN autumn a couple of years ago that I made one of the most important changes in my culinary life; I redid my kitchen in Vermont. My hyperbolic pleasure has nothing to do with fancy cabinets or luxurious tile on the floor since I didn't add any. The same simple wood-doored cabinets that have been in the house for over thirty years and the wide board floors that have been there for a hundred and fifty years are untouched. The important change was getting rid of my large everyday stove—I left the cast-iron wood stove to warm cold winter mornings and to cook the best duck I can make.

In place of my previous range, I put in a

new cook top and a separate, large oven under a nearby counter; but it isn't the shiny efficient newness of the equipment that makes such a difference.

It is the height. I am short, five foot two, and as I was planning my kitchen a little bell went off in my head. It said: "Why work at conventional height? I can put the cook top at any height I choose." There were two precipitating factors to my epiphany: The large picture windows overlooking the fields and mountains that I wanted to add suggested that if I dropped the counter, I could have a bigger window. I then thought of pictures I had seen of Julia Child's kitchen which had a caption explaining that she, tall as she is, had had her counters built higher up to make it easier for her to work. Aha! If she can raise them, I can lower them, and lower them I did.

The benefits are incalculable. Today, when I stir a stew in my large braising pot, I can see what I am doing and I don't risk what used to be a common occurrence—a red burn line where the inside of my forearm hit the chest-high rim of the hot pot. When I have to lug a heavy pot to or from the stove, I don't have to raise my shoulders and strain myself. I can hold my arms, lightly bent, out in front of me and pick the pot up comfortably. Best of all, I can see what's in the pot as it cooks.

Perhaps most surprisingly, by lowering the

cooking surface I have learned something about sex-linked characteristics in the kitchen. When I used to sauté, I was awkward. Male chefs with whom I had worked had used the recommended pot grip—overhand on the handle. I had always used an underhand grip, which is much less forceful and stable. Almost all the women with whom I had worked had done the same thing. I thought it was because we were weaker. Not at all, it was because we were shorter.

As soon as I had my new, lower burners, I could sauté with the best of them. My hand grasps the top of the handle of the skillet, my thumb toward me, and with magnificent control, I slide the pot backward and forward with a sharp jerk as I get to the far point of each slide, which makes the food neatly jump (sauté) and turn over. Victory.

Having had such success with my lowered stove top, I hacked down the legs of my butcher block. It had not escaped my notice that professional butchers were working at the same height as I then was at my proudly "professional" butcher block. Seeing their knives slash down into a side of meat, I realized that a good percentage of their strength came from the distance the blade traveled on the way down. With my amputated butcher block, I improved my power. I also had less back and shoulder pain, since my knife, the arm's extension, rested naturally on the surface of the block; I didn't have to lift my shoulder to lift the knife. I chop and mince my vegetables and herbs with the greatest rapidity and efficiency.

Based on these benefits, I began to muse about the height of things in kitchens. It was many years ago that I took my first wall oven off the wall and put it under a counter. I learned the hard way the perils of an oven too high for easy reach. I was taking a sizzling steak out from that high-up, original broiler when the heavy pan tilted in my grasp, rolling hot fat onto my arm. It was the worst burn of my life. Yes, I served dinner with my arm bound up in wet towels; I was too young to know better and take myself to the hospital.

Since I have become involved with microwave oven cooking, it has become clear to me that many microwave ovens are in equally dangerous locations. They are located high atop the stove. Every time people have to reach into the microwave, they are liable to have to reach over hot pots and food. Also, the microwave oven seals and controls are liable to become distorted by the heat.

Contrarily, despite all these successes with lower heights, I put my kitchen cabinets up high. I don't like to hit my head when working at a counter. I would rather get on a little stepladder to get my dishes down a couple of times a day.

The point of all this, I suppose, is that we tend to let ourselves be regimented by "normal" heights and standard cabinet enclosures and counters. The important thing is not what we are supposed to do because everybody does it but what works for us. Contractors and architects with their doubting faces aside, we must insist on kitchens where things are the correct height for us. We have to live with them.

THE MORALS OF PRAISE
AND PANS

WHEN I FIRST started reviewing restaurants in the early sixties, I was paid a very modest stipend and the publication never even considered paying for my meals. I was constantly in the red. I don't regret it though. I learned an enormous amount about food and restaurants.

I also learned that most reviewers at that time considered free meals provided by the restaurants an important perk of their work. Publicists for restaurants would call trying to get me to review their clients' restaurants. They were flabbergasted that I didn't take free meals.

My high moral tone—a little bit like adolescent dudgeon—was no doubt easier to maintain since I was an unknown with a far from remarkable presence and so could pass totally unnoticed in restaurants.

Today, it is commonly agreed that it is immoral for restaurant reviewers to accept free meals, free drinks and favors or, even worse, bribes whether of money or lavish presents. What one should do about being recognized and treated "specially" is argued.

Some reviewers make reservations under names other than their own and some even go so far as trying to disguise themselves—hats, wigs, etc. Some feel that, even when identified, it makes little difference as a restaurant cannot change its food, decor or wine list. Service can change; but a seasoned reviewer can look around and note the way other eaters are treated. I have found that recognition in a less than professional restaurant usually changes the service for the worse. It is tense, flustered and intrusive.

The above are fairly simple dilemmas; but recently, I have given a great deal of thought to other moral issues of reviewing restaurants, cookbooks and culinary-prose books.

I am not currently reviewing restaurants, although I may write about them from time to time in some connection. I take a review to be writing that describes an entity and then seeks to evaluate its good and bad points. In the past and even in the limited way that I refer to restaurants now, I have had some queasy moments about what should be reviewed or mentioned and how.

Some reviewers feel that they are consumer advocates whose business it is to condemn the bad and reward the good and consider these to be absolute categories. By and large, I have felt it more important to direct the attention of readers to what I thought would enhance their pleasure, to that which was notably good in some way. That value is not related to an absolute standard for all restaurants. It is part of an explained context. If a restaurant is unassuming, I do not want potential diners to think it on a par with the world's best. If a restaurant is mainly enjoyable for an experience rather than spectacular food, I think it is fair to recommend it as long as I explain the situation clearly.

Slamming restaurants just to exercise nasty wit, adjectives and adverbs does not seem to me profitable for the reader, although it does tend to make the reviewer highly visible. Only if a bad restaurant receives a great deal of promotion that might entice and then disappoint, do I think it worthwhile attacking it. A small, neighborhood restaurant without quality can perish on its own without help from me. It may, if unreviewed, survive and in some way serve a community.

A more subtle issue is the case of the good but small and limited restaurant. Reviewing it may actually kill it. A horde of eager onetime eaters may descend on the place, driving out the regulars. After the momentary fad is over, or the owners have expanded beyond their means, there may be no audience left. The pressure on the service and kitchen people may be overwhelming and annihilate just those qualities that were enjoyable. One doesn't want to review only the best restaurants; but it may be kinder to let a charming find pass by unnoticed.

Lack of notice is exactly the issue in the problem that has caused me to worry about these things again. Always, there are bad cookbooks among the good ones. Recently, there has even been a spate of nasty food books—nasty as to language or attacks on people. Does one review such books? I think not. To notice them is to give them validity. Readers' interest may be piqued; they may buy the books in search of scandal. Often readers skim reviews, not noticing that the review is a condemnation—the old, "as long as they spell your name right" publicity adage.

Reviewing truly scurrilous books is a little like reviewing pornography. My judgment is not to do it. If such books become prominent, then someone will have to take up the cudgels for honor. Otherwise, I think it best to let them die of inattention.

RECIPE OWNERSHIP

WE HAVE ALL heard a variation on the story of the cooks—Aunt Rose, old Bessie, the chef at the local restaurant—who didn't want to share their recipes. If they ever gave one out, a vital (secret) ingredient or step was sure to be missing.

I myself have been haunted by two such recipes. Oddly enough, both for cakes. The first was the most extraordinary chocolate cake I ever had—that may be a romanticized memory of childhood. All I know for sure is that it was made with German's powdered chocolate, which is no longer available, instead of flour; that it was coated with whipped cream; placed very near the ice cube compartment of a primitive refrigerator, afterward it was covered with a flowing chocolate coating—today I think it was a dark, bitter chocolate ganache—which would set up in the cold. I have never been able to get it right.

The second recipe was for a hazelnut layer cake filled with a chestnut purée that was the childhood treat of a relative. Her mother—now long dead—gave me the recipe; when faithfully reproduced, it turned out to be good, but all wrong. Something was being withheld.

My attitude toward recipes is very different, which is not simply a result of my writing them for publication, but rather the reverse. I like to share food and I find the sharing of recipes a continuation of that giving and enjoying. Obviously, many others do also or we wouldn't have had over the years so many cookbooks and reader-recipe columns in magazines and newspapers.

Sometimes I cannot share a recipe. It's not ill will. I simply have thrown a dish together out of this and that and have only a very general idea of what I have done.

The reluctance of others to share recipes may come from character, a generalized desire to control, to limit sharing, or from the cook's being famed for a certain dish and feeling that nothing else can replace this singularity and value for others. I feel that making recipes is easy and that they are all variants of the known in any case.

Why then do I get very upset when I see a recipe clearly derived from one of my own—many I can recognize as I do the faces of my children—printed under someone else's name? Why do other of my food-writer friends go off howling into the night when the same thing happens? The closer to our original, the worse our reaction; but sometimes the pilferage can be as simple as a technique that no one has devised before or the inclusion of an ingredient or seasoning that might have seemed aberrant in a given recipe before we used it and now bears the hallmark of our culinary persona.

I am not thinking here about outright plagiarism, which, in any case, American copyright law makes virtually impossible to prove. Under the law, only the actual words in which a recipe is written can be copyrighted, and it is very easy to fiddle with words. The thinking, if there is any, I suppose goes that recipes are part of a body of lore and only the words in which they are expressed can be personal property. Indeed, if somebody felt they had the copyright on coq au vin or succotash, I would also be distressed.

Additionally, I feel that my readers and all readers and users of recipes should use them only as the guidelines they really are. Cooks should vary, adapt and react to recipes—in essence, own them. No matter how I try, I can only be so exact. My lemon will not taste like yours, nor my chicken have the same savor. You will have to change the recipe.

. . . And yet . . . after all the generosity, after all the reasonableness, there are still situations that stick in the craw, and it's very hard to draw the line to make clear what they are without sounding like Scrooge. Sometimes, hubris may be a companion to arrogance and what the writer thinks is an invention or an elegant variation may turn out to be the wheel.

To try and sort out the parameters, I will use myself as a test case. Every Thanksgiving, I try to come up with a new turkey stuffing. It's a sort of game I play. Over the years, many of the prizes in the game, the recipes, have been printed in books and articles.

One year I came up with what I thought was the brilliantly original idea of using Jewish sour rye bread as the base of the stuffing. Moving on from there, I thought of caraway, which is a basic seasoning of the bread. Caraway brought me to sauerkraut. I combined all of these elements in a stuffing which did find its way into *Food For Friends*.

I was so pleased with the delicious results and with what I thought to be my creativity and originality that I called Jim Beard, with whom I spoke at least daily at that time. Excitedly, I told him of my find. Without any aura of debunking, but rather as one continuing a discussion of our mutual interest in the sources and history of foods and dishes, he said: "You know, the Pennsylvania Dutch do turkey with sauerkraut." I was mildly deflated.

I have never found the Pennsylvania Dutch recipe; but I don't doubt him. Since, I have also heard of but not seen an Alsatian recipe for turkey with sauerkraut that seems very logical.

The point of my tale is that if I had seen a recipe for turkey with sauerkraut and gotten enraged by what I thought to be theft, I might have been right, but I might just as well have been simply ignorant. If, however, I see a recipe for a rye bread and sauerkraut stuffing, I suspect I will still feel mightily abused.

In a sense, every cook who uses a recipe owns it. In another sense, some recipes are created and the parents deserve acknowledgment and praise.

FAR-SIGHTED COOKING

THE WORST CURSE for me of being an aging cook was the sudden appearance of eyeglasses—in my case, for the farsighted. Young, I had the arrogance of excellent vision and did not properly sympathize with the glasses-wearers of the world. Today, most people who need to correct their vision constantly, unless they have astigmatisms, wear contacts, which exempts them from the special glasses-in-the-kitchen problems. As a matter of fact, they have an advantage when it comes time to peel and slice the onions—less tearing.

As for me, I need glasses only from time to time—my far vision is fine and I never have the right glasses: cutting and slicing require a mild correction, the same one I use for the computer; reading a recipe requires stronger glasses, and if I am demonstrating in front of an audience, I cannot see it if I have any glasses on at all. Changing from one pair of glasses to another or shucking them altogether in between tasks inevitably means I have trouble finding them and, when I do, they are dirty with food. Attempts to solve the loss problem by hanging the glasses around the neck always result in mucky glasses, dirty and constantly needing washing.

I have had slight luck with locating glasses by only buying bright red ones. Half glasses solve the reading - the - recipe - while - talking - to - people problem, but leave unsolved the cutting one. In any case, the glasses always have a shot at losing themselves because, after having had them fog up and blind me numerous times while draining the pasta or looking in the oven to check the doneness of anything, I remove them in the probable presence of steam. (Which brings up the mildly irrelevant problem of shaving in the shower.) Bifocals are not a good solution. The correction I need, at the angle I need it, is always in the wrong place.

I have always been a lazy cook; but my recent vision problems seem to me to be influencing my cooking style in favor of the food processor and away from the knife, toward bold effect and away from precision. There have been books and monographs on artistic style being influenced by vision problems: El Greco had one awful astigmatism. How odd to think it may apply to cooking as well.

SO, YOU THINK YOU'RE AN EXPERT

> M. Jourdain: *Par ma foi! il y a plus de quarante ans que je dis de la prose sans j'en susse rien.*

> "Good heavens! For more than forty years I have been speaking prose without knowing it."— Molière, *Le Bourgeois Gentilhomme*, Act 2, Scene 4

Being a food writer is setting yourself up for a kind of double whammy. Since everybody speaks prose, everybody assumes that writing is easy. Since everybody eats, everybody assumes food expertise. In a way, it is true. We all have our own very valid sense of taste and food that we prepare or pay for in a restaurant should please us. Readers eagerly search for suggestions of where to go and what to eat. They must also read carefully for the attitudes and tastes of the writer to know if their likes are likely to mirror those of the writer. Trying a few recipes by authors whose work seems attractive will fairly rapidly tell us if their palates are enough similar to ours to warrant our trying more, buying more of their books.

Deciding where to go with its greater cost in money and potential disillusion is harder. I am often asked: "What is the best restaurant in name-your-city?" It is an almost unanswerable question. The less I know of a city, the smaller it is, the easier the response. Sometimes, I will know of only one good restaurant. Then I respond confidently. In Budapest, I suggest Lègrády Vendègló without hesitation. Even there, I am moved to add a few more names for different occasions. The problem with a city like Paris, New York, Los Angeles, London or, today, Dallas is insurmountable. When I ask in response, "Best for what?" I am seen as difficult, avoiding the issue; but I mean it.

Do you want French, new American, Chinese, Japanese or Italian food? If Italian, northern or southern or nuova cucina; how can I compare disparate cuisines? Do you want a gala, spectacular place with impeccable service where decor counts, or do you want the kind of place that I go to repeatedly with pleasure? Does price matter? How can I compare the charm and good food of an old bistro like Chez Benoît in Paris to the splendors of Robuchon? Robuchon is best if there is an absolute standard; but I probably go to Benoît more often.

When it comes to recipes, the conflict between subjective taste and the reality defined by the written word remains. Readers and cooks in America expect a great deal of precision . . . no "season to taste." I have taught cooking classes where I will throw some salt into a dish or grind some pepper on top of it. Invariably, some frantic student will ask: "How much did you add?" This means that, as much as we value our own personal approach, we seek a defined reality that cannot exist.

In my books, I try to tell people a good deal about the ingredients they are using. I explain that my lemon and your lemon will give off different amounts of juice and that that juice will vary in acidity, sweetness and sometimes, unfortunately, acridity. Certainly, olive oil and vinegar will vary wildly from kitchen to kitchen, and that variation will enormously change the final flavor of the dish. I could drive people crazy by specifying a brand for each ingredient, many of which they might have trouble finding. Instead, I confide myself to the taste buds of the cook, hoping that gentle indications such as a fruity olive oil will help.

Cooks will confront me variously with "can I add a little cinnamon to that custard?" or "I always put cinnamon in mine" or "how can you make that without cinnamon?" No matter what the tone, my response is "if you like it, do it." Sometimes the suggestion is worth my adapting; sometimes, it just doesn't suit my taste.

With all of my reservations, I have not yet come up with an answer for times when people ask me what my favorite recipe is in a book. I find that I can't tell them that I like them all.

PASSIONS AND PEEVES

DOWN WITH AL DENTE

AMONG MY CULINARY gripes is one
that may have been caused in part by us, the food
writers, as we called for fresh, crisp and al dente. If
I want a raw carrot, I will eat one. I don't want a
raw carrot heated in butter. In California, I have
been served undercooked eggplant, a literally nau-
seating dish. While tiny, fresh garden peas are sensational raw, the larger peas available in stores taste
floury unless fully cooked. Haricots verts—tiny,
round French string beans—develop neither their
best color nor full flavor when merely blanched.
They need to be thoroughly cooked, although not
to grayness or mushiness, in order to be fully ap-
preciated. An aside—what is the affectation that

tops but does not tail these same green beans? It may look pretty, but the tails are fibrous, not good eating. At some point, we need to correlate looks with taste. Foods need to eat well. While most fish must be left slightly undercooked so as not to be dry and often tough, the newly popular monkfish has to cook longer than normal if it is not to be rubbery. I agree with Jeremiah Tower of San Francisco's Stars that most cooks underdo sweetbreads. They need a longer cooking with aromatics to become flavorful and have a pleasant texture. By all means keep the asparagus crisp, but don't give me crisp beets.

Indeed, some vegetables in some kinds of cooking are meant to go far beyond even what I mean by proper cooking. In parts of Italy, older string beans and broccoli are often slowly cooked for a long time, providing a delicious flavor and one quite different from usual expectation.

Similarly, although I tend to like and cook lamb rather rare, I would not try to make a Greek or Turkish lamb dish by keeping the lamb rosy. It would be inauthentic; but more important, I would be missing a unique flavor.

Well, I've vented my spleen; but it is important to think about cooking not just follow mindless slogans.

IN DEFENSE OF CANNED TUNA

A SHORT WORD for canned tuna fish, one of America's great contributions to the world of food, and, no, I am not jesting. I am not about to make an attempt to bring back tuna-noodle casserole, occasionally topped with cornflakes, but I will stake my gastronomic laurels on the fact that tuna salad makes one of the all-time great sandwiches. In the effort to defend canned tuna, I sometimes give my own recipe for tuna salad. This requires that we note that not all canned tuna is created equal. I am not, however, talking about fancy French tuna, in cans like those for sardines, packed flat in olive oil; although this is also a great delicacy and hard to obtain. Nor do I mean the

55

very good Italian tuna packed in olive oil in conventional round tins—expensive and strong in taste. What I do mean is fancy, white albacore tuna solidly packed in either water or a neutral oil, both of which are discarded in any case. Beware canned tuna in chunks, which tastes like dry, shredded, limp cardboard.

Too often, I have been assaulted in restaurants that think themselves very à la page with salade Niçoise containing fresh tuna. Usually, it is very badly cooked. Even when it is well cooked, fresh tuna does not have the rich, slightly mysterious flavor so necessary for the enrichment of this dish. Canned tuna is also essential for various Italian dishes. These are the recipes in which to use Italian tuna. Cannellini beans with tuna and red onions, pasta with tomato, olive and tuna sauce, and tuna in antipasto are all unthinkable with fresh tuna.

It is all very well for all of us to learn about relatively new ingredients. The many varieties of fresh tuna are well worth enjoying. That does not mean that we have to insult and demean staples that we enjoyed in a more innocent time. Especially, as in the case of neat cans of tuna, we can have them waiting on our shelves when need arises. Long live canned tuna.

MODEST ERUPTIONS

IN A WORLD where a glass of white wine has become the standard apéritif, particularly in restaurants, I am out of step. I prefer red wine and am mildly paranoid about much of the white wine that has climbed into undeserved prominence on the wings of increased customer demand. A lot of the white wine served at endless receptions, bars and restaurants, anonymously, by the glass is undrinkable and acidic. I have gone back to asking for a vodka watered by lots of ice or a Scotch and soda—which have no more alcohol or calories and can be nursed longer while staying cold.

There are responsible restaurants, restaurants that are proud of their wines-by-the-glass and tell you what they are; but I still prefer red wine and am perfectly happy to start drinking it before the meal begins. The problems then are with friends and the menu.

I am not alone among many of my friends. Most of the serious food people I know would rather drink red wine and are relieved when I suggest ordering a bottle at the beginning of the meal. Other friends and mere acquaintances, however, may feel imposed upon. This is even more true when they are choosing to eat fish or chicken. If I suggest red, they look at me askance. Yes, I know it's not standard; but I like red wine with salmon or roast chicken. I would draw the line at oysters. If more restaurants would carry a good selection of wines in half bottles, the problem could be solved: I could have my red, my friends their white.

The real problem is due to current attitudes toward healthful eating and the response to them by chefs who are already, on the better and more au courant menus, creating primarily seafood or fish- and chicken-based foods, often with lots of acid and sharp seasonings that are hardly ideal accompaniments to good red Burgundy, Bordeaux, Piemontese or California wine. In the new bistros and informal restaurants, there will be a steak for the retrograde fifties customer that I willy-nilly become. (By the way, I do not consider a filet mignon a reasonable steak. It is tender; but it usually has no taste.) The death of real prime beef makes meat healthier and leaner, but eliminates the succulent flavor and rich texture provided by extensive marbling.

If, at least, restaurants were able to maintain cheese in good condition, I could have my red with that. Alas, the small demand and the legal requirements to keep cheese refrigerated make it almost unavailable in restaurants. If you couple that with the insane restrictions on cheese made with raw milk, you will see how grave the problem has become. I don't want anybody to get listeria, tuberculosis or any other disease that comes from raw milk; but aged cheeses—and it is these in which pasteurized milk so decisively changes the aging and the flavor for the worse—become safe after many months of aging. Countries where aged, raw milk cheeses are eaten don't have health problems from this cause.

While I am ventilating irritations and prejudices, I might as well confess an un-American loathing for pasta salad. I enjoy Chinese cold noodles and cold Japanese udon as much as the next person; but most of the bastard, slimy, cooked, pseudo-Italian pastas dished up with bits of ends of vegetables and ham or shrimp swimming in oily vinaigrette or mayonnaise are inedible and tasteless. There is such a thing as adapting foods beyond their natural limitations.

I have another set of cranks connected with pasta. We seem to drown our pastas in sauce. Good pasta should have a flavor of its own and should be lightly coated with sauce, not masked and with a puddle of sauce lying lonely at the bottom of the bowl. If the dish doesn't have enough flavor, the answer is not to add more sauce, but to increase its intensity, perhaps with more reduction or with heightened seasoning—another clove of garlic, a smidgen of salt, some red pepper flakes or chopped fresh herbs.

Also when waiters come waving grated cheese at you, don't automatically say yes. Cheese does not belong on every sort of pasta dish. It doesn't belong on linguine with white clam sauce and almost never on any pasta with seafood. Fresh or raw vegetable sauces sometimes have their flavors muddied by cheese. In many cases, the ideal but seldom observed way to add cheese to pasta is to toss it with the cooked pasta before sauce is added. This gives the cheese a chance to cook slightly and blend into the finished dish.

The quality of the cheese that you use is the most important in the simplest preparations such as fettuccine with only butter or olive oil, salt, black pepper and cheese. Whatever the pasta you are making, don't sprinkle cheese out of one of those red-and-green-decorated containers from the supermarket. Buy a good, aged piece of Parmesan and grate it into a little water reserved from cooking the pasta or into a little olive oil and stir right onto the drained steaming pasta at the last minute.

You are replacing sawdust with flavor. There are good hand-held cheese graters that make it easy, or take an old-fashioned four-sided grater, put it on a plate with a hunk of cheese and let each guest grate his own. A nice napkin in which to hold the cheese is an added touch.

Even if the pasta dish you are eating in a restaurant warrants cheese, taste the dish before letting the waiter add cheese or adding it yourself; the cook may have known what to do. If the cheese is in a bowl or shaker on the table, taste to make sure you will be adding a fresh, good flavor. There is no need to let habit make us restaurant victims.

A FEW LEAVES

I REMEMBER THE fifties when news first began to arrive in New York about San Francisco salad bars. My first courier was a jazz musician friend who couldn't understand their absence in New York. Since I had a couple of years earlier been introduced in Cambridge, Massachusetts, to my first McDonald's, another California import, I was less than ready to be thrilled. Additionally, I had never taken to the great American habit of salad before the meal. I don't think salad is something to fill you up so that you cannot enjoy the main course. Instead, I like it as a way to clear the palate after the main course.

Had I foreseen the depths and putative

heights to which the salad and the salad bar were going to sink and soar, I might have taken to the warpath.

Salad bars litter our restaurants and are, in exchange, littered with imitation bacon, chemically treated vegetables and soggy, browning lettuce that gives iceberg (Simpson) a bad name. At the other end of the spectrum, it has become difficult to escape from an upscale restaurant without a badly dressed salad—drizzled not tossed—topped with a heterogeneous mess of ingredients. The California version has become a few elegant leaves with hot but not melted—it doesn't melt—goat cheese.

Sitting at a gastronomic competition for young chefs a few years ago, I became amused by the trendiness of the ingredients that were being used, and I decided to invent a salad using every then current gastronomic cliché. After I started, I confided my game to the other judges and they entered into it with glee. The salad would have a base of radicchio and dressing made with raspberry vinegar. The toppings would include goat cheese, macadamia nuts and kiwi or mango slices. Extra ingredients such as breast of quail and wild mushrooms are ad lib.

Part of the blame has to be borne by the French. There was a time when the visiting French were contemptuous of the American habit of eating salad first, particularly when it contained what they would consider extraneous matter—even tomatoes were considered in this light, although a salade tomate—tomatoes, olive oil, salt, pepper and herbs of choice—was deemed perfectly all right as a first course.

Then the French fell in love with the salade gastronomique, and it became hard to leave even their best restaurants without leaves topped with a plethora of expensive ingredients. Criticisms of American habits were forgotten along with the lovely green leaves in their rightful place.

When I think of salad, it is not your fancy salade composé filled with every luxury from crayfish to foie gras, nor the pasta salad once developed to use up restaurant leftovers and now creeping into homes to replace the far better, cool, molded salads of the thirties, nor yet your main-course mammoths: the chef's, Cobb and seafood, although I can occasionally be deflected from the desire for a plain green salad by a lavish, well-made Caesar salad.

What I really crave is that petite salade verte that you used to get automatically at the end of every normal French meal. It had soft green leaves of basic Boston lettuce, today called—I suppose more fancily—butterhead lettuce in seed catalogues. It was what the French generically called laitue. The dressing was simple: oil, vinegar, salt and pepper. There might be prepared mustard or garlic, and, from time to time, in places that were trying a little harder, some finely chopped parsley, fines herbes or a spoonful of whole, fresh tarragon leaves.

I am rarely a dessert eater. To me, salad is still the perfect ending to a meal, perhaps with a bit of good cheese to finish the bread and the wine. It never just arrives anymore. Often, I will make a special fuss and get a waiter and kitchen to produce a salad while my sweet-toothed friends are eating dessert. I always have to fight to keep my bread and butter. I am living witness to the death of a tradition destroyed by the birth of the fancy salads.

American habits are more understandable than the French transformation. Traditionally, we didn't eat a first course. The salad was just a filler before the meat and potatoes. It may be that growing interest in Italian and French Provençale food contributed to the trend. The Italians have always made me happy with wonderful salads of tiny string beans, tomatoes and an optional sprinkling of finely sliced white onions. This, however, did come in the proper salad position. The southern French had crudités and salade Niçoise as starters.

All the understanding changes nothing; I want my salad and I want it after my main course.

LOVING LEFTOVERS

I'M THE ORIGINAL eater of the odd breakfast: cold spaghetti, the piece of cake I never have for dinner, the tuna salad that didn't fit into yesterday's lunchtime sandwich or a leftover bowl of soup. These leftovers are just minor dividends, on-the-run snacks, as are the leftovers my kids mean when they rummage through the refrigerator and complain petulantly, "There's nothing to eat"; although the refrigerator is full of staples: eggs, milk, fruit and vegetables. What they want is not an ingredient, but something already cooked and full of flavor, to eat cold or hot, as is.

The leftovers that I celebrate are the bits and pieces that can be made into new dishes, the home cook's version of the restaurant chef's mise-en-place. Some of the best dishes I've ever made were happy accidents cooked from this and that: These are the recipes that tend to look so complicated when I try to write them down for another cook.

Such dishes can sometimes be spotted by the length of their ingredient list and the preparation, which takes two or three steps. I've often suspected that the multiple variations and complexity of many famous recipes such as cassoulet or salade Niçoise are a happenstance of some other cook's leftovers.

I must confess that one of my more complex recipes and one of my son's favorite dishes—one he even makes for his friends—artichokes with snails and beurre blanc would never have had beurre blanc (refrigerator cold) as an ingredient if it hadn't already been lurking in the refrigerator. I had bought the artichokes, but decided I wanted a more festive presentation than boiled. The snails, cream, white wine and mustard were all on hand. The rest evolved.

A dish that fancy is not an everyday event. What is a more typical picture? It's dinnertime and I haven't the foggiest idea what I'm going to cook. "Look, there are a few stalks of cooked broccoli left from yesterday's dinner. I know there was some skim-milk ricotta left when I made lasagna on Monday. There must be frozen chicken stock. Was there some cooked rice? No; but there is a leftover baked potato. Who was that woman with Alfred, the one on the diet who wouldn't eat her potato? Never mind. I have the makings for soup." The cheese, the broccoli and peeled potato all go into the food processor until they are mush. I whisk them together in a saucepan with the broth; heat, season, and serve.

My children, like generations of French children, were raised on potage, a soup made with various vegetable assortments, put through a food mill and heated with stock, tomato juice, milk or even water.

Often I have a carrot from a bunch that didn't get used, a stalk of celery, half of an onion and some extra chopped parsley—I didn't use it all a day ago. There may even be some cooked mushrooms or pesto. From there to a version of minestrone is a short trot with a can of tomatoes, possibly some broth and some boiled pasta.

Leftover cooked rice gets turned into an impromptu version of fried rice. Leftover cooked dried beans can go into soup—whole or mashed. Mashed, they make refried beans or extend a meat loaf. My recipe for veal with letcho arose because, after a trip to Hungary, I made letcho (a melting concoction of red tomatoes, red peppers, onions and paprika) to serve with eggs for a brunch. Now I make it and keep it in the refrigerator.

It is one of the deliberately made leftovers, called staples, that I have learned to keep on hand.

Now that my microwave and I have become such good friends, I can make more of these leftovers in short order. My freezer is stuffed with containers of the cook's version of Linus's security blanket, stock of all kinds, as well as tomato purée and sauce and duxelles.

My microwave means that I can quickly cook baking potatoes so I don't have to depend on leftovers. They turn up in many of my recipes. The infinite varieties of potato salad are a legacy from generations of cooks dealing with leftover potatoes. Croquettes are a use for leftover mashed potatoes, which also make a good room-temperature salad with mayonnaise, chives, crisp bacon crumbles, onion, celery seed and salt and pepper.

Hash, chef's salad and chicken salad are tributes to leftover meats which can easily go into a new stew with cut-up leftover vegetables, microwave-cooked potatoes or other vegetables, some broth and new seasonings such as onions, garlic and herbs.

Since I love my leftovers, I have been confused by their bad name. Certainly, they embody frugality. Maybe that's the problem. We associate them with poverty, with the days when there was a roast on Sunday and its leftovers turned up barely disguised—slathered with white sauce, swimming in pallid soup, chopped in hash, or simply served in a cold slab with bottled sauce or relish—all week as dinner. Overcooked boiled chicken or beef used to make soup suffered the same fate. That was truly unnecessary. Most of the energy of the stock comes from the bones. The beef or chicken can be put in long enough to cook until just done. Then the meat makes really good leftovers.

When America came out of the Depression and its poverty and World War II and its restrictions, the country discarded its leftovers with relief. Fresh became the new password for quality. This seemed to rule out leftovers; but that was nonsense. The ingredients that originally made those leftovers were fresh, and there is nothing wrong with them a day or so later. Besides, the best chefs I know are thrifty, putting trimmings from vegetables into the stockpot and saving necks, wing tips, gizzards and even the gnawed-on bones of cooked birds—they will be boiled—for the same pot.

While some leftovers such as soup or stew may be perfectly good—indeed better—the day after, others we need to rescue with imagination, or they will be greeted with that despondent sigh, "Oh, leftovers." I expect to continue to regard my trove of leftovers as a treasury of labor-saving starts on a new meal.

TAKING FOODS'
TEMPERATURES

YOU HAVE ONLY to taste a sorbet frozen
so cold that it sets your teeth on edge, causes the
spoon to stick to the tongue, and defies the most
talented to savor much of the flavor to know what
I mean when I lament that recipe descriptions of
the temperatures at which foods are to be served
are extremely imprecise. The proper temperature
for serving food and wine has much to do with the
pleasure of eating or drinking.

The two most common adjectives are
"cold" and "hot." "Cold" does not inform me that
I want a "cold" meat to have cooled off, but that I
do not want it straight from the refrigerator. It
must have enough of the chill taken off so that the

internal fat is unctuous and flavorful. "Cold" also doesn't indicate that drinks should be frosty; but soup—though hardly the room temperature of the roast meat—should not be cold enough to congeal the cream that may be in it. The ubiquitousness of refrigerators and hot summers is no excuse for serving poached fish so cold that it is tasteless.

While salad greens should be crisp—unless purposely wilted, or fatigued, in the style of older English and French recipes—they should not be gelid. Fresh out of the spinner or towel is the ideal solution; but if washed salad is kept, as I keep it, in the refrigerator for convenience's sake, it is kinder to the eaters to take it out of the refrigerator a half hour before tossing it with dressing. The dressing is another concern. If it is kept in the refrigerator, take it out when taking out the greens. Oil that is cold doesn't flow or coat properly and is the next thing to tasteless. Raw tomatoes should always be served at room temperature. Cucumbers can be cold if you prefer.

As someone pointed out to me when I recommended that we encourage restaurants to make soup again by ordering it, the soup often comes to the table at a temperature that can only kindly be described as tepid. Having worked in restaurants, I understand that the soup is often kept warm in a bain-marie and picked up by a waiter rather than being served forth hot, portion by portion, by a cook. This is an unfortunate practice, since the soup reduces in the bain-marie and the seasonings go out of whack. Also, some soups—crystal-clear consommés and the comforting hearty soups of winter—need to be steaming hot when they arrive in front of us, with the steam carrying the inviting aroma. Of course, egg-and-cream-bound soups cannot be that hot or they will separate or curdle. That is not an excuse for elegant frigidity unless we mean to serve vichyssoise.

While I'm on things that deserve to be served steaming, every cup of tea that I get in a restaurant is lukewarm—which is not even to mention the nasty bit of paper that signals the presence of a tea bag. I do not think it too much to ask that pots that have been left to get warm with hot water inside be served with boiling hot tea prepared from loose tea. This requires a strainer; but gratitude from tea drinkers will be immense. Then we can try to extend the idea to chamomile and herb teas; it will be bliss.

I also bemoan, for caffeine-addict friends, that coffee is kept in a state of permanent suspension on warmers that present it neither fresh nor hot.

On the other hand, it should be remembered that if the food is so hot that it burns, our pleasure will not only be over immediately, but also we cannot taste at the very hottest or coldest points on the scale. Since metal spoons get hot or cold in the food, the aesthetic Chinese and Japanese provide spoons of china or wood for hot soup. The wily Victorians, inventors of untold table implements, had spoons with sawtooth fronts to their bowls so that ice cream could be tasted on the front of the tongue rather than cold metal. An epicurean friend uses a fork with success.

At home, we have more control over the temperature at which we serve things; but given the limitation of recipe description, a little thought may be required.

The recipe writer has a problem in English with dishes that are supposed to be served neither hot nor cold but warmish. The proper words would be "tepid" or "lukewarm"; but their frequent use in English to mean insipid or wishy-washy seems to poison every dish to which they are applied. Without the burden of these meanings, French restaurants and books can use the silky-sounding word tiède happily, as in salade tiède (usually implying that a goody like sautéed foie gras or a welcome but more plebeian alternative like sautéed lardoons top the greens, which may themselves be lightly warmed)—or is that just my snobbery speaking?

Wine, however, should not be lukewarm. Room temperature does not mean that your Bordeaux should be the temperature of your July room—unless bitterly air conditioned. Even in winter, our current notion of comfort is much too warm for wine. The temperature that was intended when the phrase originated was the temperature the wine would achieve about a half hour after it was brought from a fifty-five–degree cellar into a stone-walled room that was lucky to be as warm as sixty-five degrees.

Consequently, I have startled if not dismayed waiters and nearby wine snobs by asking to have very good red wines chilled slightly (certainly not to the briskness of a Beaujolais).

White wines, including Champagnes, particularly the good ones, are not supposed to be chilled into insensibility when they can neither be sniffed nor tasted by chilling to a point just above freezing. Traditionally, they were taken out of that cold cellar and served at that temperature. The ice bucket, if any, was there only to ensure that the wines got no hotter.

So I add to your difficulties, but I hope pleasures as well, by encouraging you to consider what is meant by cold or hot when you are preparing food. If food—soup for instance—is not the right temperature in a restaurant, send it back for adjustment just as you would a miscooked steak or piece of fish.

IT'S ALL RIGHT TO EAT

I LIKE TO EAT. There, I've confessed.
Perhaps if I go on prime time television with my
confession, I will be forgiven. Some may call me
an addict. It is true; I cannot do without food.
Worse, I enjoy the way it makes me feel. Ridiculous ideas? Not really. Food has come to be
seen—at least in public—as a foe. We are chastised
for our weight, our cholesterol, and for eating
tainted foods.

I'm as much for health as the next one.
However, I think that it's important to remember,
in our harried search for vigor, that food should be
a happy idea. The scare headlines have gotten out

of control. Food will not kill you. Doing without is what does us in.

Sometimes it seems as if there is nothing left that we can eat without dire warning. I used to say, in years past, they were going to discover that mother's milk is bad for babies. We have gone beyond the joke.

Let's face it: Food is one of life's great and dependable pleasures. The more we care about the flavor and cooking of our food, the more we respect it instead of scarfing it down mindlessly, the more likely it is that it will be healthful and delicious and so will we.

All the rules can be made pretty simple. Buy good, fresh food. Go back to the old notion of a balanced diet without eliminating any group of foods. Eat more carbohydrates—breads, cereals, beans, legumes, pasta, rice and potatoes—vegetables and fruit. Eat less animal flesh, including fish: as little as three ounces a day is about right. Limit the butter and eggs. Don't eat too much.

The overwhelming majority of us are not killed by our food. It's safer than it used to be for most of us. Yes, it's a good thing we no longer get typhoid fever from milk. Of course, we don't want chemical sprayers polluting our food any more than we want poisonous waste in our waters. Let's by all means lobby for sane regulations and testing where need be—mainly so that we don't have to obsess over foods.

I still eat raw, briny oysters and clams with ardor. That is an admission of gluttony, a certain point of view and the knowledge that cooking the seafood will not make any difference. You cannot cook clams and oysters long enough or to a hot enough temperature to kill pollutants unless you like to eat rubber bands. I do buy my seafood from the best stores and check it to make sure that it is fresh.

It's been many years—sadly—since I dug a clam; but if I were going out with bucket and shovel tomorrow, I would check with the state to make sure I wasn't digging in a polluted area.

I haven't given up on chickens. I can cook them long enough and get them hot enough so that they will not give me diseases. I am willing to spend more to buy organically raised chickens and eggs when I can find them. They taste better as well as having fewer contaminants.

Similarly, I search for local, small-farm—raised organic fruits and vegetables. I see in their visual imperfections old-fashioned virtues of freshness and flavor. If I buy good, naturally raised tomatoes—not those bred to taste like cardboard and endure jostling travel like iron—I can be sure that they will have enough acid so that my canning jars don't turn into land mines.

As to diet, in the sense of weight control,

some of my thinnest friends are the dessert eaters. They eat, but not to excess. Overweight is one of America's major health problems; I think that is because we love our food too little, not too much. If it tastes fabulous, if every bite delights, if we really pay attention, we will end up eating less, not to deprive ourselves, but because we will be satisfied.

A green salad of varied leaves lavished with just enough (toss well to coat, not flood) virgin olive oil, some lemon juice or balsamic vinegar, a little salt, pepper and perhaps a sprinkling of herbs tastes splendid. That it is better for us than soggy coleslaw from the deli, or salad-bar greens limp with oddly flavored bottled dressings, goes without saying. It is better for our souls and our bodies; it is rich in vitamins and monounsaturated fat—the good kind.

If we eat well in the sense of flavor and pleasure, we will also eat well in terms of health. Let's get back to the main business of food—cooking and eating.

FOOD FADS

I FIND IT hard to account for food fads. In retrospect, some seem logical: Yes, everybody loves potatoes and finds mashed potatoes the ultimate comfort food in a nostalgic period. Why, however, have we been through a sudden rush to mashed potatoes? People argued over the merits of different kinds of potatoes for mashing and over the relative virtues of creations indecently rich in butter, or those silken with olive oil, or the ones divinely homemade in flavor and airy in texture lightened with hot milk and a bit of butter.

Once fads get started, it's easy to see how they steam-roll. Inspiration or pure imitation clots the menus. Sea changes are suffered. England, in the grip of the same mania, stressed the homey, nostalgia element with poor people's dishes like bubble and squeak—potatoes mashed with cooked cabbage—turning up in fancy restaurants, and Paul Levy of *The Observer* defended lumps.

Nor did the passion cool alongside the mashed potatoes. We have seen on both sides of the Atlantic thinly sliced, crisply sautéed potatoes used instead of puff pastry to sandwich fish and/or vegetables. The ultimate push may have been an all-potato menu in Saulieu. Five courses were varied by the type of potato used, the cooking method and delicious additions such as black truffles or a reduced oxtail essence. Nothing was too good for the potatoes.

I love potatoes; but the fad got out of hand even though their basic lure cannot be dimmed. There are other foods that cannot be killed by fashion. They endure. Some dishes, like pizza, pasta and pita, turn from fashion to staple. Others have a moment of glory, are tortured by increasingly obscure variations until they die in disrespect and then are set for a comeback, like quiche. Still others, like kiwis, have a brief moment of fame and ubiquitous chic. Then they disappear from trendy restaurants and food articles, but live on in people's homes, selling more than they did in their fashion prime.

Szechuan, Tex-Mex, leading to "real" Mexican and Cajun could all have been (and were) predicted. They all rewarded a search for spicier flavors; the American foods were part of the turning homeward that came with a politically more conservative, less expansionistic era. Some, like guacamole and gazpacho, had been paving the way for years. Sometimes, only one item from the hit parade of a chosen cuisine lasts, as was the way with Paul Prudhomme's blackened redfish. For a brief moment, every food in America was being blackened, often to a hideous charcoal-black mouthful of ashes.

The recent turn to bistro food in France and America also has a logic. This food is less expensive and less demanding. It's easy after a harried day. Why was it deemed that the ideal accompaniment to bistro food, French or American, was a mountain of fried potatoes? I know they are called French fries and we all grew up eating them; but the French do eat other things.

Why have some foods not caught on? Certainly, Indian and Middle Eastern cuisines provide a rich and varied repertoire of flavors with plenty of spice for those who seek it. Yet they have remained the province of the serious cook, the experimenter.

Based on the recent flood of immigration to our shores, I thought that we would see a boom in Russian and Caribbean foods. Certainly, new peoples bringing their dishes, planting and selling the needed crops and staples, making restaurants and gradually having their food pervade the national larder and menu has been a part of the history of food trends in America. Perhaps I am merely setting too short a time frame, and soon callaloo, cherimoya and acras, along with pelmenyi and winter borscht, will be staples on our menus.

Whether the actual dishes invade our lives or not, we are sure to see the ingredients and flavorings with which they are made popping up on trendy plates. No chef worth his salt these days seems to be able to resist a new ingredient. I would watch for Southeast Asian lemon grass to pop up in unlikely dishes—I like it myself—along with tropical fruits so far undreamed of. This is already happening in the more elegant restaurants of Miami, the Southwest and California.

Other trends are hovering about waiting to happen. The return of fifties food is one. Chicken à la king, once the bane of the banquet circuit but very good when well made, chocolate pudding and even molded tomato aspic are all good bets. Look for recipes using exotic grains, some very old like millet and others, like quinoa, new to us but old in the Andes. We have been told to increase our carbohydrate consumption; but that isn't going to limit the foodies to potatoes, pasta and bread.

However, you may see a resurgence of sixties-style, multi-grain bread baking. What's good doesn't die; it just waits a while to be a new trend again.

When it comes to trends, I have some small sense of how it feels to be an astrologer. It is not that I read the stars. But at the end of each year, or shortly into the next one, magazines and newspapers from around the country start calling to find out my culinary predictions for the year to come. By March, I have read my prophecies with as much discomfort as I made them. I really don't believe that people change the way they eat as they change hairstyles. When American regional food popped up, for example, it was clear that it would be with us, in some manifestation, for a long time. I look forward with terror to the forecast-frenzy of the millennium.

SAUCE SPOONS

FOR SOMEONE who loves a good sauce down to the last unctuous drop, doesn't like to thin its taste by sopping it up with a lot of bread and is capable of skimming it up on an errant finger, to the disapproval of all and sundry, there is a nineteenth-century French utensil that I love—the sauce spoon. The spoon is very flat so that you can elegantly scrape along the surface of the plate in search of final treasure or make sure that each mouthful of food has its share of sauce. It's more elegant than my fingers.

NOTES FROM THE RESTAURANT FRONT

THE MYSTERY OF
LEMON PEEL

I HAVE A culinary mystery: How did the
nasty bit of lemon peel get on the saucer of the
espresso cup? I remember being young and very
impressionable, out with a man who seemed to me
at that time the apogee of sophistication. Come
coffee time, he carefully showed me how to twist
the strip of peel and at the same time, with a lit
match, flame the drops of essential oil it exuded
over the coffee. I was instructed not to drop in the
peel. Subsequently, I became less impressionable,
traveled to Italy, discovered that no matter where
I went there was no yellow next to my espresso. A
little thought made it clear that the lemon added
nothing. When you compound the unnecessary

with the horribleness of the thick pieces of peel that are everywhere the case, with lots of bitter white pith on them or slightly dried from age, I think it is time to stamp out the peel.

By the way, now that all sorts of restaurants have espresso machines and are even making de-caffeinated espresso, it would be nice to try to get them to make ristretto. That is the dense coffee extract you get in thimble-size cups in Italy. It is made by forcing less steam than usual through the grounds. It is restrained, ristretto. That is my favorite coffee, and since the steam is so slightly on the grounds, you get full flavor. Let's campaign.

DISHONORED
RESERVATIONS

SEATED IN A minuscule chair at 10 P.M., having a drink while waiting to have a 9:00 o'clock dinner reservation honored, it occurred to me forcibly that nothing can ruin a good meal as quickly as a badly handled reservation. Being intelligent, you may ask why I was still waiting after such rude treatment. Well, I had struggled up a minor Caribbean mountain and, it being a busy time of the tourist year, I knew another good meal could not easily be had at that moment. I have been in the same situation in New York and, on a Saturday night with a group of waiting friends, been boxed in as well. It is scant revenge to know

I will never return to such a restaurant. There is no way of getting even.

I have worked with restaurants enough to know their problems: the table that sits endlessly over a single cup of coffee, the table that arrived a half hour late for its reservation and, perhaps most aggravating of all, the reservation that was never canceled; the people simply didn't appear. It may be little wonder that restaurants overbook and keep me waiting. All the understanding in the world doesn't make it pleasant. Fifteen minutes is an understandable wait—nothing longer. Good restaurateurs manage the problem.

Maybe if we all resolved to honor our reservations on time or cancel them and if we kept our acquaintances from making multiple reservations for the same night so they have last-minute options—yes, there are people who do that even under different names to avoid discovery—maybe we could get restaurants to behave and everyone would be better off.

A REAL GRIND

A PEPPERMILL WAVED over my plate by a zealous waiter just after the food arrives is an amenity gone amuck. When—I hope politely—I ask to taste the food before I decide if I want pepper or not, the peppermill wielders look nonplussed. It is clear that they see no relationship between the proferred pepper and the way the chef has seasoned the food, which may tell you a lot about what they think of the kitchen's cooking. I like pepper, but not everywhere.

ENOUGH SAID

ONCE UPON A time you knew you were in a fancy restaurant because the waiters were professionals. They seemed born with their black garments, shuffling walk and deferential manner. Many spoke Franglais. Non-fancy restaurants had their menus written on wall-affixed blackboards. The waiters were either tired versions of the fancy restaurant's waiters or members of the owner's family.

Then, the nature of waiters began to change. In New York, Los Angeles and London, many seemed to be out-of-work actors, and taking an order became increasingly an audition. Restaurant owners have contributed to this nonsense, instructing waiters to introduce themselves to you: Hello, I'm Victor, your waiter. Friendliness cannot be scripted and the best service is unobtrusive. I'm not a casting director, nor am I in need of new best friends.

As the personnel changed, the menus changed as well, with many more daily specials to pique jaded appetites and give scope to the creativity of a probably young chef and his interest in fresh, seasonal foods. Gradually, the waiters added to their general act a set performance of a long list of daily specials.

In a restaurant where the audience is not composed entirely of regulars, a long recitative of specials slows service unbelievably. There are various problems. If the waiter tells you the specials when the menu is presented, most of them are forgotten before the menus are read. Then, a complex discussion goes on as various people try to remember whether the lotte (monkfish) had the wild mushrooms or whether that was the veal, and so forth. If the waiter lists the specials when coming to take the order, inevitably a scramble goes on as people change their minds. Even after the order is given, there may be a lingering sensation that something critical has been missed.

There may also be discomforts about money. In response to a growing tide of consumerism, particularly from food writers, waiters in many restaurants have been instructed to recite the price of each dish. This sounds awkward and diners are seldom self-confident enough to ask for repetitions.

If the food is unfamiliar either because it is very inventive or because it belongs to a cuisine—Cambodian, for instance—unfamiliar to most, the waiter's star turn is prolonged by explanations.

In restaurants with this format, the diner and the kitchen are heavily dependent on the tastes and enthusiasms of the waiter and on the extent of the waiter's ability to communicate. Why then not get rid of this time-consuming confusing performance? Well, some waiters enjoy it and there is no doubt that specials sell disproportionately well. My current suggestion is that menus be printed in a format that can be changed easily, frequently and inexpensively, with date indications so that guests get a sense that everything is a special. It may still be necessary to have two verbal specials; but I think that should be the limit.

I don't really want anybody doing auditions at my table no matter how charming they are, nor do I enjoy the endless discussion that goes: Now, Susan was having the shrimp—not the shrimp on the menu but the special—and Albert was having the regular shrimp; no, he was having the lobster special—did that have coriander?—then he will have the veal; now, what was in that? . . . and so forth.

What I do want the waiter to know and to be prepared to talk succinctly about is what is in the dish and how it is cooked. Enough said.

SELLING YOUR BIRTHRIGHT

FINDING A MESS of pottage (a good lentil soup) is getting harder and harder. Soup, as a category, is virtually disappearing from restaurant menus; and I feel that I am being deprived of my birthright, the steaming bowl that comforts and sustains. Yes, I make soup at home. I find that my friends, who must have been scared at birth by a stockpot, don't.

Italian restaurants will generally provide something they call minestrone, although it is usually no more than a minestra di verdura, vegetable soup. When pressed they may offer a bowl of stracciatella—more watery than brothy—or tortellini in brodo. They offer these because they can quickly be made with what's on hand. The ubiquitous zuppa di pesce should contain bread to be a "zuppa"; but the bread is always missing. It's an assortment of seafood gilded with sauce, not soup.

The rich, regional peasant soups that sustain life, from the well-known pasta e fagioli to meatball soup to simple vegetable soups, like those with cabbage, are nowhere to be seen.

If you go to a French bistro and look for the erstwhile omnipresent potage of puréed vegetables—once peasant breakfast and dinner—it is not to be found. Or look in vain on the most elegant of French menus for the crystal-clear double consommé that was for centuries the test of a great chef's skill. It had to be perfectly transparent, rich in flavor, silky with natural gelatin from the bones and judiciously seasoned. Bisques and cream soups have gone the way of the dodo along with peasanty, sustaining potato and leek soup.

It used to be that every respectable restaurant had to have at least three soups: a clear soup, a cream soup or bisque and a thick, manly soup such as pea or lentil. In warm weather, the consommé could turn to madrilène and the cream soup be chilled. Today, the plague of "fresh" that has deprived us of deep-tasting stews seems to have taken its toll of soups, the bases for which must be made ahead. I like fresh as much as the next one when it comes to salad greens, vegetables and fish; but there comes a time when the chefs have to go into the kitchen more than a few hours before dinner if they want me to be happy. When I'm on a diet, it's consommé I want as a first course; when I'm chilly and hungry, it's a rich, full-flavored soup. I have gotten to the point where I am willing to judge restaurants on their soups.

While Southwestern, Mexican and new California restaurants generally provide some kind of bean soup on which they pride themselves, I look in vain for caldo michi (an aromatic rather than hot fish soup) or sopa de lima (a very spicy chicken and lime soup from the Yucatán).

It is possible to go to restaurants of some of the less popularized ethnic cuisines and find soup. The Thais, for example, have not abandoned their wonderful dom yam gung, a hot-and-sour shrimp soup with fragrant seasonings, or coconut chicken soup, a spicy chicken soup with lemon grass—with a variety of names, variants on gaeng dom yam— the biblical basil, hot peppers and ginger.

When I attacked my French restaurant friends with what I consider their serious dereliction of duty, they told me that they ceased to make soups because no one ordered them—which doesn't seem to have stopped the flight to fame of Robuchon's chilled gelée of cauliflower with caviar. If it sounds odd, take my word for it; it's sublime. Michel Guérard still sells pots of his lightened crayfish bisque, which is a taste memory for anybody, even though I still mourn the incredibly rich version that he used to make at Le Pot au Feu in Asnières before he got the religion of health.

Isn't it perverse that people don't order soup, since they are always complaining about restaurant prices, and soups are among the less expensive offerings and are loaded with nutrition?

The nutrition element is not to be sneezed at in an era when the government is telling us to eat less meat and to increase our carbohydrates and various fibers. Soup is the logical solution, filling us up and filling in the holes in our vitamin intake.

Maybe if you do what I do and ask about soup in restaurants that you visit, we can bring good soup back. The reviewers among us can start paying as much attention to soup—or its lack—in our reviews as we do to the chefs' more obvious set pieces.

At home, soup is as easy as cans of chicken broth kept on the shelf near some pastas— orzo, pastina, vermicelli—or cans of beans. The ever-ready clove of garlic or onion bulb—very healthful—and odds and ends of vegetables and herbs quickly make soups that can be a whole meal.

If you have a little more time, consider broth quickly made from scratch in a microwave oven and stored in the freezer to be used as needed. Bake a potato; cook up a vegetable or vegetables of your choice from carrots, onions, broccoli or peas to sweet potatoes, spinach, acorn squash, watercress, fennel, celery or parsley. Put the whole thing in a food processor or through a food mill and there you are. If calories are not a problem, enrich the finished soup with some olive oil or yogurt, or even a little butter, cream or grated cheese.

If there is nothing else on hand, salad greens can be cut up, melted in a little butter or oil and cooked with onions and broth to make a light soup. Escarole is traditional; but almost all will work. Remember the leftover cooked vegetables or bits of meat. Otherwise, they are often forgotten in the back of the refrigerator, until sanitation requires eviction.

Don't neglect that can of tomatoes on your shelf. The contents, puréed with some chicken broth, herbs, and skim-milk cottage cheese, can be quick and satisfying. When using canned tomatoes, always consider perking them up with a little fresh lemon juice. The lovely acidity from the tomatoes dies in the canning process. The lemon juice replaces it.

Spices like curry or chili can lend interest to anything from split pea soup to potato or carrot soup. Just be sure to cook the spices first in a little oil or their flavors will be raw. Black pepper and salt should be added only at the last minute.

BABY HOURS

IT SEEMS TO me that in all my eager expounding of future trends, even though I predicted and then observed the current, modest baby boom, I missed an obvious clue to the twenty-year-distant what's-to-come. Now I note changes in child-rearing patterns. Working parents today no longer force reluctant babies and small children into bed at a ritual 7:30. The mothers and fathers want to see their children when they can, even if that means setting up a high chair at a dinner party or letting conversation be deflected by a toddler among the cocktail glasses. I have been jealous of the relaxed pleasures of these parents.

I first became aware of the new schedule in

child-rearing when I noted strollers, babies-on-banquettes and infant seats of various kinds in rather posh, if not the most formal, French restaurants in the evening—not the roadside Howard Johnson's at lunch. Nevertheless, I missed the obvious inference: We are raising a generation for whom family and pleasure are meal- and restaurant-oriented. We may feel today that the obsession with these things has become disproportionate, yet we may live to see this new group even more food-centered than we are.

There is one very positive side to all this. Amid much press attention to the decline in family eating and the growth in numbers of people living and eating alone, it is good to see kids being included and to hope that they in turn will see communal eating as one of life's happy norms. We in this country retained—as we citified and gentrified ourselves away from the farm—a vaguely Victorian notion that children did not belong in restaurants or at dinner parties. It always amazed me that French, Italian and Chinese children all behaved with perfect propriety at table while American kids seemed to racket around, unable to sit still. The answer, now, seems obvious: They had no early training.

So, despite the fact that we are surrounded by doomsayers, I am positive and hopeful. Some of you may remember with me the forties and fifties. I contend that we eat much better today, have a clearer idea of what good food is, than we did then. It would also be impossibly elitist to extol an earlier past in which a substantial proportion of the population was at the starvation level or to laud a diet that was incredibly stuffed with animal fats, even as I wax nostalgic for much that was good—farm-fresh foods and long-simmered, aromatic soups and stews—in the world's past.

PAST PERFECT

AGAINST PROGRESS

I KNOW IT'S practically un-American to be against progress. Nostalgia's permitted if no one takes it seriously. To tell the truth, I don't want to give up my refrigerator, dishwasher and self-cleaning oven. I don't even want to abandon my food processor, blender, microwave or this computer on which I write.

What then provokes the cranky title of this essay? I was in a trendy new restaurant the other day and paid fifteen dollars for eggs and bacon, a dab of home fries, toast—no jelly. That's the meal I used to get at a lunch counter, without fuss and for about two dollars. Norman Rockwell, where are you now?

I miss all those places I used to go for a simple meal at reasonable prices. Schrafft's with its impeccable club sandwich is gone. My neighborhood has gotten so chic there is no more blue-plate-special greasy spoon. The soda fountain has become a chain or a clothing store. There is no place to get a real fudge sundae with the fudge kept hot in an eternally simmering pot emitting come-hither smells at the end of a marble counter.

When I go to an unknown city, I have to ask where to eat. There is no more slipping down to a nearby ladies' lunch place for chicken salad, a glass of iced tea, and a piece of creditable pie or the surprising, fluffy white glory of coconut layer cake. What has happened to a good egg salad sandwich?

Getting to any city ensures an assault on taste and stomach whether by rail or plane. There used to be trains with real dining cars with crisp white cloths, tiny new potatoes and baby lamb (both from Colorado), good soups, good service and good coffee. Traveling alone, there was enough light to read by—missed today in restaurants as well. Going by car, where are the diners with ample plates of homemade food? The remaining few have become landmarks to search out. Even the Howard Johnsons of old were better than today's disappearing disappointments on the edge of the road and in malls.

In cities where walking is still acceptable,

wander down the street at three o'clock of a fine afternoon and try to get something to eat. The local five-and-dime used to offer a sandwich of grilled cheese that melted, with a little cup of good coleslaw and a soda. Lunch counters and soda fountains offered empty booths—not overly comfortable with their straight backs and metal-rimmed tables—and a decent feed. The Automat is gone and cafeterias have acquired the bad reputation of school lunchrooms. Even hotels are giving up their coffee shops—never very good—in favor of higher-priced, if no better, restaurants.

To eat at three o'clock today requires a Chinese restaurant or putting the appetite on hold until four, when some trendy place will be serving a pale imitation of English tea; but gone are the tea shoppes d'antan.

These little deaths mean that what used to be American staples—hash, french fries, cottage fries, mashed potatoes, pot roasts, chocolate layer cake, lemon meringue pie, ice cream, coleslaw, potato salad, grilled chicken, a good hamburger, a chef's salad, a BLT, a substantial soup of the day like mushroom barley or chicken rice that didn't come out of a can, and fried clams that were whole bellies lightly floured and freshly fried with a tangy tartar sauce instead of pre-prepared and doughy clam strips—have all become the province of upscale restaurants that cannot let well enough alone. Their chefs must tinker to prove that they have earned their keep. Some things are not improved by innovation.

The other locus is fast food, which is a major death for any food I like. Think of doughnuts that were really meant for dunking, hamburgers—rare and juicy—or fried chicken that was light and crisp.

The alternative is probably cooking at home; but there are some foods that I do not want to cook at home. I do not cook the fancier creations of elegant restaurants. I leave to them the dishes with three sauces or the sauces made from three bases—on hand for them, but not for me. I do not turn vegetables, make puff pastry or arrange individual plates of hot food. Similarly, I want my hot pastrami in a deli and accompanied by sharply acid, drippy pickles that don't come out of a plastic bucket.

Yes, I know there are still delis; but most of them get their meats from a central supplier along with their sweetly tasteless coleslaw and potato salad. Even tuna salad has become mass-produced, pasty glop without acidity, texture or freshness.

Give me hashed browns off a griddle and flapjacks browned beside them that are not made from a mix. What has happened to the crisp waffle with warm maple syrup? On comfort days in sloppy clothes, I don't want macadamia waffles with exotic grains.

These are the foods within most memories.

I also remember hearts of lettuce—yes, iceberg—with Russian dressing and good, thin watercress sandwiches. Imagine my horror a few years ago when I went to an old-time and once fancy pastry and tea room in Manhattan and was served, upon request, a watercress sandwich. Placed before me was a plate with two slices of commercial white bread, crusts on. The slices were separated by a whole bunch of watercress, stems and all. The hot chocolate I had ordered wasn't made with chocolate but a sweetened mix and the whipped cream on top was airy and ersatz, not dense and faintly golden with rich cream. Bah, humbug.

I understand rising rents and rising labor costs; but I miss having a shoemaker on the corner and a butcher I can talk to and learn from. Let's be careful to cherish the simple places that remain to us before they disappear.

THE REAL PAST

COME THE WARM, ripening days of summer and I imagine that I am closer to a more ancient, basic and healthful style of vegetable and grain eating than in my cold and meaty winters. I am seduced by my garden and neighboring farm stands vivid with color and flavor.

I avoid a lot of hot time in the kitchen. Much is eaten raw or almost: vegetable soups—gazpacho has many names and many recipes—vegetable sauces for rice or pasta and endless salads. I have corn on the cob and other vegetables in every form: grilled, roasted, steamed, stir-fried, puréed and combined in a variety of stews to be eaten hot, cold and at room temperature. Fresh herbs, garlic, onions and imagination sauce the dishes. The first beans from the pod or dried beans, fruit, cheese, bread and wine complete my menus.

There is almost no meat and little chicken or fish—an occasional grilling, a stew more vegetable than meat, a slice of cold meat or charcuterie, a boiled egg, a little tuna from the can.

I eat this way for pleasure as well as in a modern quest for a more healthful diet. Those who came before us ate this way to take advantage of what they had—often limited. While we tend to see a cornucopia-vision of the past, rich in more seasonal, more natural foods, it is only partly true. Winter in most climates was short of fresh vegetables, and the world relied on salting, pickling, drying and cold storage for any vegetables at all. The animal protein we are fending off today was in short, expensive supply.

With the best will in the world and without an evil intention, food writers and the natural inclination of all of us to glamorize the past and the far away have been guilty of distorting our view of the way the world eats. By selecting the best, the most festive food of other places or times, we have come to see them as halcyon visions of plenty, filled with meat and seafood, sugar and cream.

It is not sugarplum fairies, but roasts and fries, sausages and sautés, stews and cassoulets that frolic in our Rabelaisian dreams. Southern picnics are enriched with baked hams and fried chicken.

Clambakes clutter the shores of a mythical New England. In that world of the imagination, native Africans are awash in chicken and ground-nut stew, native Americans feast on venison and buffalo, Greeks expand over countless dishes of succulent lamb, the Chinese are exquisite in damask while dining on unimaginably choice viands.

The English eat hearty roasts, silken salmon and mountains of oysters. The French of the mind are various, either robust peasants, glorying in rich stews or jeweled aristocrats whose famous chefs set forth succulent sauces. Our Italians live in a world of perpetual holidays, their risotti topped with pungent white truffles.

While not totally untrue—these foods did exist in each of these countries and were eaten by the natives at least upon occasion—such visions falsify the totality of real experience and may contribute to the glut of fat and cholesterol in our lives. We equate these festive foods with good living and think that, if we can, we should eat this way all the time.

Our ancestors and many peoples all over the world today eat very differently from this skewed perception. Carbohydrate, or stodge, was what really fed and filled up most people. With bread as the staff of life in Europe, scarcity led to bread riots for centuries. Even in the recent past, when the government-fixed price of bread was raised in France, the announcement was carefully scheduled for August when almost all Frenchmen are on vacation.

Certainly, the staple food of the vast majority of the world is still rice, followed by bread and potatoes along with noodles—pasta among them—soy foods, yams, taro, yucca, corn, beans, pulses such as lentils, myriad grains and other starchy foods with names foreign to me. In the past and in much of the present, animal protein, when available at all, has been primarily a flavoring.

Beasts were not killed promiscuously. They were the cash crops and the providers of the milk and eggs. If a pig was slaughtered in the fall, that was a major event, and a family would hoard the preserved hams for Christmas and Easter, or sliver small amounts for a taste at many meals. A prosciutto bone or other ham bone was an asset to be used and reused in soups until flavorless. Fresh meats were rare; only the overage animal or the single, religiously festive springling was sacrificed.

To envisage a chicken in every pot was to dream of luxury indeed—the most luxurious of Sunday dinners.

If other meats were salted and smoked like bacon, or pickled like corned beef, air-dried like grisson or jerky, or preserved in fat like confit, it was to keep them over the winter and dispense them parsimoniously as special treats.

So when we read recipes for peasant dishes crammed with meat, we should remember that we are reading about rare treats, not daily fare. Even fishing nations could have uncertain catches, rough seas and months when it was impossible to put out upon the water. Even plenty might need to be sold. A home-cooked paella was mainly rice, seasonings, oil and vegetables.

The great go-along-withs have been vegetables and fruits, fresh when in season, pickled or preserved for inclement times. A little fat would have come from the possibilities of each region—olive oil, butter and lard. Food was about survival and pleasure when possible. No one got more than a nutritionally sound share of meat and fat over the course of a year. It is these daily recipes that are by and large missing or recorded primarily as accompanying dishes in our cookbooks and kitchens.

It is up to us to re-create out of our plenty the sane eating and pleasures that scarcity and invention, herb patch and garden, bestowed on our forebears.

ON THE SIDE

GREAT FRENCH RESTAURATEUR-chefs keep bistros on the side as I am told— some things are before my time—affluent Frenchmen used to keep mistresses. These bistro-mistresses are not the grandes cocottes who frequented Maxim's but the shopgirls whose simplicity and, one assumes, earthy sensuality presumably provided a respite from the formality of bourgeois living.

The bistros, then, are the shopgirl-mistresses, a relief from the formal demands of star (Michelin) status with simpler, earthier food. The best one I have been to was Au Petit Comptoir, the plaything of Gérard Boyer of the three star restaurant-hotel, Les Crayères, in Reims. A restaurant without tourists, the bistro carefully evokes past years, with wood, etched glass and red ginghamlike wallpaper with a floral border, sturdy china in dark green with a gold rim and sturdy low-stemmed glasses, and is frequented by the professional class of the city.

It is wonderful, as good in its way as his 'Les Crayères.' No nonsense at the Comptoir about small portions with tidbits carefully arranged and vegetables on the side. There, ample amounts come with a starch from tiny white beans called cocus alongside a braised pig's knuckle and plenty of spoon-worthy gravy to those gutsy sausages, andouillettes, served with a sauté of pommes Lyonnaise. A potato gratin is a specialty, and the first course of marinated herring, onions and carrots is served over warm pommes à l'huile, a sort of hot potato salad.

I guess that the last few years' fuss over potatoes in the upper echelons of French gastronomy were leading up to this loving bistro return.

The bistro is not just a relaxation. It has had to be rescued by fine chefs, because the old bistro with its regular customers, dingy cream walls, mirrors and bar is disappearing, or, as in the sad case of Allard, where Madame used to cook so lovingly, is being sold and exploited. The food is cooked without love or care.

I suspect that the joy with which customers

are welcoming bistros in this country as well as in France is not primarily a question of lower prices. The restaurant goer wants value. He or she can grill, broil and sauté expensive ingredients at home. Out we want either superb cooking with elegant sauces or traditional long-simmered and full-flavored dishes we do not have the time to make. Some of these dishes are being adapted, refined and served in very elegant restaurants.

The first such dish I had was several years ago at the Moulin de Mougins: a pied de porc that was boned, stuffed with foie gras, wild mushrooms and truffles, and cooked to unctuous beauty. I have now seen similarly extravagant versions at a good selection of great French restaurants, and in America cooked by Gérard Pangaud; the meat is taken entirely off the bone, shredded and served wrapped in caul fat. One was at the two-star Apicius in Paris where I had the best tête de veau of my entire life. I have had three-star tête de porc, and Philippe Groult of Amphyclès, a stellar Parisian arrival, makes a joue de boeuf that is even better than the ones in the classic bistro, Benoît.

There are even regional variations of these upgraded bistro dishes. At La Bourride in Caen, which is in the heart of Normandy, I had a superb meal, the centerpiece of which was a fresh pig's knuckle simmered in cider until it was mahogany brown, tender and slightly sweet with the perfume of apples. This was served with a timbale of thinly sliced cabbage sautéed until just soft, potatoes and tiny lardoons.

Much as I welcome this trend to traditional food, there are a few trend-breezes stirring that make me a touch anxious. Since trends hop the Channel to England and the Pond, as the English call the Atlantic, to America with dazzling speed—I had herring with potatoes as a tiny, free first course at the very excellent Tante Claire in London—it might be well to warn you.

· Those free tastes that used to be hors d'oeuvre and then were amuse-bouches or -gueules have become patienters, things to keep you patient, which seems a little more literal than necessary especially as it is only in the very best restaurants such as Le Crocodile in Strasbourg— where I had a lightly fried tiny roll of fish from the Indre served with the world's best sauce tartare and an oyster in aspic with dill on a tomato sauce—that these dishes are either original, tempting or able to make me happy to wait.

While the dill was perfect with the oyster, I have noted that dill and anise greens are replacing chervil as the ubiquitous garnish, not always felicitously.

Fish keeps being touted on the menu as rôti, which should mean roasted, but instead seems to mean a fillet that has been warmed in the oven with too much olive oil. That reminds me: Today, the olive oil is on the fish and the nut oil is on the salad, where it is often much too strong a flavor. I don't know if the olive oil on the fish derives from Italy; but it is a trend that needs stopping. Olive oil on its own or even with a few herbs is not a sauce.

I'm fairly sure that these wanton name changes and culinary variations are partly responsible for the return to foods with recognizable names. A mistress is one thing, a harlot is something else.

MULBERRY MOMENTS

WHEN I WAS growing up, the grandmother of a friend was the most elegant woman I
knew. Clad, always without a wrinkle, in various
mourning shades—grays, lavenders and blacks—of
silk chiffon, a matching veil around her almost
white hair, she would be driven with us, in a
matched caravan of bottle-green Packards—
limousine, touring car (convertible) and estate
car—all garnished with tiny apricot roses in cut-
crystal vases, to her house on the bay. Voluptuary
and posh as these experiences were, they paled beside a delight that awaited arrival.

In the old-fashioned garden of the house,
beyond the glass-enclosed summer living room

and between the rose borders, stood two mulberry trees I now know to have been weeping mulberries, whose trailing branches almost brushed the ground between the sprays of dark leaves. Two little girls in white summer dresses, heavy dark braids slapping on their backs, could stand in the "green shade" and begrime themselves—stained fingers, blackened tongues and teeth and, invariably, spotted dresses either from our hands or from the gently plopping berries.

The taste as we rushed berries from tree to mouth was extraordinary, sun-warmed, wine-intense rich juice popping from berries tongue-crushed against the welcoming palate. Sated, we would fill flat wicker baskets—flat so the berries wouldn't turn to instant juice—with full-ripe berries and take them to the Hungarian cook, pale with steam and flour from her baking.

Later, I reconstructed her special mulberry strudel and began to think of a multitude of ways to use these spectacular and neglected berries for cooking. The past's legacy was well worth preserving.

Normally, mulberries are a rare seasonal delight since the fruit travels badly; their savor is reserved for those who have trees or whose friends with trees are generous with the abundant berries. To preserve the taste for other times, make a mulberry syrup. It keeps virtually indefinitely.

I have just planted two trees of my own.

FAMILY SUPPER

THE WORDS FAMILY supper carry with them an almost unutterable nostalgia, images and emotions of past times wrapped in a vague glow of pleasure and better values, the generations meeting for a sharing of food, conversation and affection. Norman Rockwell paintings, Laura Ingalls Wilder's books, large linen napkins, grandparents, Southern verandas, paneled dining rooms and vast deal kitchen tables combine in the imagination with arrays of roasted birds and joints, homemade breads, jams and pickles, assorted vegetables and a ravishment of pies, cakes and cookies. The board is not only laden, it groans.

Sadly, as the end of the twentieth century

approaches, we rarely have time for these ritual meals. Many children have two working parents. We eat out and send out more than those grandparents; but we should not, nor do we, abandon one of the few times we have with the yuppie puppies.

Our tastes are more sophisticated; we are more concerned about the healthfulness of the food we serve; kitchen time may have shrunk to well under an hour. But we still can share laughter, the day's joys and woes and good food. We can create our own memories that remind us that we are families, not just people living in the same house.

Rescuing the warm past shouldn't revive the clean-plate-club and hassles about "drink that whole thing," or "no dessert until you finish the Brussels sprouts." Children seldom starve themselves. Try putting all those vegetables into the comfort of French-style potage or cut them up raw—small children seem to eat anything they clutch in a fist—and serve with a nice messy, mushy dip as a starter. Put the milk into puddings and other desserts. Avoiding "yuck," which can ruin any meal, may mean avoiding spicy food, even though Mexican and Indian children survive. The alternative is not bland; season so that you enjoy the food and so that your children learn what good fresh food is.

Children accept what exists in their own house as normal. A set table, a lighted candle, real glasses shimmering in their light and no cartons anywhere—the dishwasher has to run anyhow—turn eats into supper. I always serve a salad with dinner. Now, my children are addicted and that's healthy. By keeping washed greens and a simple dressing in the refrigerator, it's easy.

Meals with more than one course mean less eat-and-run, more tastes and delights, better nutrition and more sit-and-talk-about-the-day. They can be done in a reasonable time by using a microwave oven, a wok, a sauté pan and the broiler or grill along with a food processor, a mixer, a blender and judicious shopping. The goal is not to be fancy or to show off. We can cook good simple meals that won't exhaust the cook. Let's bring back home and hearth—if available—and a good roast chicken.

Children can participate in making the meal. If the kitchen is a place to enjoy together and is not a chore, children will help and grow up to have an interest in good food.

SO THERE, TOM WOLFE: GOING BACK HOME TO ENTERTAIN

THERE WAS A time in the eighties when I was sad, if not outraged, that America seemed to be giving away its tradition of hospitality. It didn't seem that anybody was saying, "Come on home for dinner," our gracious legacy from a frontier society. Instead, people went out to vast and noisy halls purveying something like food. Everybody was eating in restaurants as if they had forgotten what a kitchen was. Seemingly, they were searching for distraction rather than intimacy. But this is a more conservative time, and home values are beginning to look a lot better. We are staying home more, entertaining more, drinking less. Whatever the reasons, I enjoy the results.

I cherish a fantasy in which I have a maid, a butler and a cook. The maid is wearing a black uniform—a dress, not pants, made of cotton, not synthetics, that has a starched lace and organdy collar—and serviceable shoes. The cook is at work in a vast, clean, neat kitchen with a deal table and perhaps a fireplace. Dinner is ready. The butler is checking the table setting to see that the silver is properly polished, and I am in my bathtub amid scads of bubble-bath foam waiting to emerge into a bias-cut satin dress.

Listen, it's my fantasy. In it, I can have a perfect body and slink down to Jean Harlow's *Dinner at Eight*.

Neither I nor most of the world lives in this soap bubble; but we are staying at home anyhow.

Partially, the reasons are demographic. The population bulge—the median age—has hit over thirty-four for the first time ever. When you consider that a substantial number of the souls under thirty-five are the children of the new baby boom, you can see just how overwhelmingly important those over–thirty-five families are. They are staying home because of those children. Children are the world's most expensive hobby. If the parents have some kind of child care during the day so that they can go to work, they can rarely afford it at night. Besides, they want to see that precious—often delayed—child or children occasionally.

When they get home, they get dressed

down for play. They don't want to dress up and start out again for dinner. In any case, restaurants have become very expensive. Getting older may also call for less kicks and noise and more quiet and comfort.

Perhaps most important of all, the constant diner-out has begun to realize that eating at home is not only cheaper and possibly more casual; but it is a better way to be intimate, to have conversations and to relax.

Those who have developed a taste for good wine realize that they can have more value for their dollar at home.

If everybody is going home again, it's not to the same food, the same kind of entertaining or the same level of formality that their parents or grandparents enjoyed. Entertaining, like everything else, may have skipped a generation.

Certainly, the homes of today are smaller and entertaining has changed. What is needed today is parties where no help is required. Remember help?; everybody used to have it; nobody does anymore except for the glossiest occasions.

We often need parties where children can run around. They aren't put to bed at 7:30 anymore so "Mummie" can have a quiet drink and dinner. Maybe my fantasy household needs a nanny, at least Nana, the dog, from *Peter Pan,* or Mary Poppins. Did you ever stop to think that, although Mr. and Mrs. Banks are repeatedly described as poor, they had, in addition to Mary Poppins, Mrs. Brill the cook, Ellen, the maid, and the inefficient Robertson Ay, who blacked the boots so badly.

We are seldom at home like Mrs. Banks was. We have jobs, do community work and get our exercise, in addition to taking children to the endless places children seem to need to go. We want foods that can be fixed ahead, or foods that can be hurriedly put together at the last minute.

Where an early generation would have served a standing rib roast (and very good it was too before we knew so much about cholesterol), we serve foods from every place under the sun. French, Italian, Mexican and Chinese are daily fare, and so we take flight to more exotic regions for inspiration.

Moroccan seasonings are rich and satisfying without breaking our budgets. Today's Indian curries—not the cream curries of a simpler time—served with lots of rice fill us up, can wait if need be and, slightly modified (avoid the coconut), can be very healthful. We cook fish as a main course and dish up pasta for openers. We have begun to conquer our microwave ovens and know that some frozen and canned foods—chicken broth, tomato purée (the best comes from Italy in sterile cardboard containers), frozen peas—can be helpful staples.

A big salad and a good piece of bread can

elevate any meal. I would like to see us try what used to be "home" foods—not for company—like really good chicken à la king or New England boiled dinner. Maybe as we move briskly backward in time toward gracious entertaining, it will happen. In the meantime, a roast chicken with a crackling skin and stuffed with herbs and lemon or a roast leg of lamb with mashed potatoes are quick and comforting. It's the kind of food you cannot get in restaurants. Everybody eats it happily at my house.

Time isn't an issue, because I roast the meat at five hundred degrees Fahrenheit, and then let the oven clean itself. There is something to be said for today.

WHITE GLOVES AND ICE CREAM

THERE WAS A time, which doesn't seem so long ago to me, when you went out to get ice cream unless you were prepared to crank in a spilling slush of ice and salt. Iceboxes were still being filled daily with blocks of ice and sawdust. Refrigerators were new, but selling rapidly, even mid-Depression. However, their freezing compartments, usually suspended from the top of the interior, were tiny, barely large enough to hold two small ice-cube trays. Ice cream placed there melted quickly into a messy puddle.

Going out for ice cream was a gala event, except for the rare summer cone, sugar of course, dripping down a hot, salty arm at the beach.

Dressed up on a winter Sunday afternoon, I would go out with the grown-ups. I was buttoned into a scratchy blue tweed coat with a velvet collar and revolting matching tweed leggings if the day was very cold. I had on white gloves, which I was supposed to keep clean. Seated in the ice cream parlor around small marble-topped tables on tippy, wire-framed imitations of bentwood chairs, my coat removed, I was silent as the grown-ups talked and very aware of the elastic holding on my Breton bowler which cut into the defenseless skin beneath my chin. Bored, I swung legs that did not reach the floor, kicking the cast-iron center leg of the table. When the soda or sundae arrived in its high, special glass dish, I would stretch as tall as could be so as to get the straw in my mouth, or to use the long-handled spoon to scoop up gooey bites of sundae. It demanded infinite care to negotiate the perilous trip from glass to mouth with melting ice cream if I was not to disgrace myself.

Less self-indulgent grown-ups ate single scoops, often conical, of ice cream in fluted metal containers. Either stuck into the ice cream or on the side were thin, crisp, waffled wafers, sometimes with flavored cream inside.

Soda parlors were luxurious with marble or tile floors, stained-glass windows and lamp shades. Even modest ones in drugstores existed amid the glitter of glass apothecary bottles filled with mysterious red and green fluids and Latin-decorated ceramic jars traced in gold.

Sometimes, alone with a single adult, I would sit on the tall, swiveling stools at the soda fountain. My hands gripping the round, cool edge of the marble counter, I would turn myself dizzily from side to side until strictly adjured to "stop that." The fountain was awe-inspiring. Darkly carved and mahogany, it sparkled with beveled-edge pier mirrors and shining brass or nickel soda heads, a marvel of Victorian excess. No, I'm not that old; but there were still some around when I was a child. There are even a few still today. Many have been turned into bars.

At particularly posh children's birthday parties, ice cream arrived from the caterers multihued and molded into naturalistic peaches, miniature pineapples, bunches of grapes and fruits I had never seen. More appropriately, there were clowns with pompoms on their hats and baby animals; rabbits, chicks, puppies and lambs. Adults' black-tie dinners had multilayered bombes. One layer at least was frequently a bright pistachio green. This was the era of mile-high pie and baked Alaska. There are some things I'm glad haven't come back. The molds for all these desserts—two-part lead molds for the fancy shapes, and tin molds with a removable cap at the top to release suction when the mold cover was released for the bombes—have become costly collectors' items.

Gradually, freezers in home refrigerators increased in size, and Louis Sherry disappeared from the scene as an elegant caterer and ice cream parlor, its name surviving on cardboard ice cream packages. Before they had gone, Schlumbom's, the West Side New York soda fountain of my childhood, had disappeared.

In my early adolescence, particularly in the country, Howard Johnson's was a place to go for a date. High school kids didn't drink, at least not in public. All over the country there were—some survive—favorite local ice cream parlors and they were great dating places. Exaggerated sundaes to feed two or a crowd, although some boys boasted they could finish one all by themselves, arrived on the scene. We were wearing bobby sox, huge sweaters and no little white gloves. There were banana splits, a fitting dinner for a cage of monkeys, as many as eight kinds of ice cream, five or six kinds of sauce—usually hot fudge, butterscotch, strawberry, pineapple, marshmallow and sauces so odd in color it was hard to tell what they were—whipped cream, chopped nuts, perhaps multicolored sprinkles, and certainly a topping of a bright red cherry.

There was a whole language for ice cream, much of it regional, all of it hotly defended. A milkshake in New York was a frappe in Boston, a cabinet in Rhode Island. My sprinkles were my friends' jimmies. Some would accept only chocolate; others opted for a wild variety of colors, leading in an extreme case to round silver-coated dots the size and shape of the little red dots, occasionally heart shaped. I never could understand the salted peanuts that turned up on some concoctions; but perhaps I was just getting too old.

Gradually, life became somewhat less like a Doris Day movie. Beer not ice cream became the order of the day. Ice cream was something you ate at home.

Even the grown-ups had stopped wearing white gloves. The elegant ice cream parlors were in trouble. Rumpelmayer's had tea, but not much ice cream. Hicks survived due to a genius counterman, later to surface on his own as Mr. Jennings. Schrafft's began slipping from the scene. Drugstores found that they were making more money on cosmetics, perfumes and, finally, small electric appliances than on their soda fountains, and the soda fountains lost.

Everybody went on a diet. It's not clear if they lost any weight; but ice cream sales went down. The fast-food chains sold us tankers full of imitation ice cream drinks. Ice cream cones turned into cardboard. Fewer children were being born, and the ring of the bell on the ice cream truck was no longer greeted by prototypical children with freckles and braids or brush haircuts. No one was being discovered at Schwab's fabled drugstore and, finally, it closed. We were getting what seemed to be pretty sophisticated.

Well, a funny thing began to happen. People began to collect ice cream parlor chairs for their homes. A few cautious new parlors opened in the fancier suburbs. Premium brands of ice cream began taking over more and more of the market. Manufacturers of small kitchen equipment came up with better ice cream makers. Some of them didn't need any ice, let alone rock salt. Friends in Chicago air-mailed me chocolate-covered ice cream bars on dry ice. College students returning from Cambridge spread the word of a strange ice cream parlor where they mushed the ice cream and mixed in all kinds of goodies. The idea turned into a chain. Ice cream even turned into a socially conscious food—politically correct ingredients and rain-forest-encouraging indulgences. Rumors began to run through the foodie population of surviving small makers of premium ice cream. Elegant restaurants now serve old-fashioned ice cream sundaes to substantial sales. We had lost something and we wanted it back.

With little effort we can produce our own sundaes with premium ice creams we make or buy. What is required are fabulous sauces, sinfully rich and fresh, and unsweetened whipped cream. Remember to serve long-enough spoons—iced-tea spoons are good—so that the sauce that pools at the

bottom of the dish can be brought lovingly upward to eat with the ice cream. I wouldn't dream
of suggesting how you eat an ice cream cone. All
of us have our own ritual. Mine culminates by
ducking my head under the cone, nipping off the
pointed tip and sucking out the remaining ice
cream.

THE SUN IN ITS MOTION

"Things by season season'd are"
—The Merchant of Venice

GREEN HOPE

GREEN HOPE IS that ideal moment of planning a garden and ordering seeds, of visualizing perfect beds with ripe vegetables and no weeds. In the mind's garden, no plant has been blighted by a late frost, wilted by forgotten watering or tortured by invading insects, animals or funguses. From this garden comes just the proper proportion of perfect vegetables, burgeoning with flavor and color and no awkward gluts of overgrown zucchinis and radishes gone woodily to seed.

Faced with my catalogues in late winter, I forget past disappointments and disasters. This is the gardener's perfect moment of the year before the peat pots, sieved soil and seedlings sprouting under the beds' warmth.

These are the plans that will lead to a summer with soups, stews, curries, pasta sauces, baked, grilled and pickled vegetables, and fruit desserts—often raw—and jams, preserves and jellies. I will put up, freeze and pickle until I have to buy a second refrigerator-freezer. I like the pickles kept cold and crisp. Freezing is self-evident.

Some past wisdom does invade my plans. My garden grows—if not flourishingly—in the cool country of southern Vermont with a short growing season. Predators that are less insistent or are absent in more suburban areas still thrive around me. Moles, badgers and deer are at the ready for tender shoots, and the wily raccoons almost defy my stratagems. I have sunk chicken wire to defeat the burrowers and erected an ugly electrified fence to hamper the deer.

I know that my short, intense growing season will give me radiant fruit better by far than that from gentler climates. From the first wild strawberries picked nose-to-the-earth through rhubarb, Montmorency cherries—bright red and acid-perfect for pies and jellies—to cultivated strawberries, currants, gooseberries, raspberries, a half dozen sorts of plums, pears of every variety and an abundance of apples. It is not every year that I get ripe peaches and apricots, but often enough to make them worth growing.

I have given up lamenting my inability to grow artichokes, or——out of doors——figs, bay and rosemary. I make do with lovage, parsley, chives, lavender, savories, oregano, marjoram, mints, tarragon and many kinds of basil and thyme. My knot arrangements of thyme are often spotty with the holes of dead plants that didn't make it through an arduous winter; but the creeping thyme happily compensates with carpets of colored leaves and flowers.

I may be more patient with my struggling perennials than those in kinder countries are. I welcome back every sign of new foliage. No matter how stunted a plant may look, I give it time and care.

Dreaming of warm days to come, I make a pact with the future by planting tomatoes and snapdragons for late summer and fall pleasure. It is time to drag out the egg boxes and sacks of sterile potting soil that make the cellar look like an annex of the Collier brothers' old apartment.

A needle stuck through the bottom of each egg hollow creates a hole for drainage. The promise of the coming smell of a warmer outdoors enriches my still chilly air as I mix the soil with water and use it to fill each hollow. I shake each gaudy packet so that the seeds are in one corner, tear it open and spill the seeds into my palm before poking one or two into each prepared space.

This ritual used to be so entrancing that I

145

prepared more plants than I could fit first under the bed and then under my growing lights. Even those plants I could fit gave me more vegetables than I could water, let alone eat or preserve—how much zucchini can you manage to give away?

Now I choose carefully. I no longer grow corn. Neighboring fields are covered with stalks whose perfect ears are sold at local farm stands. It was the raccoons that defeated me. No matter how well fenced the garden, just as the corn ripened, when the morning came when I said, "Today, we will eat the first corn," I would go out to find the ears shucked, the kernels all stripped cleanly away from the cob, grasped in the night by sharp-clawed paws, lined up with their husks in a neat, arrogant, heartbreaking row.

I no longer grow most of the standard tomato varieties to put up in quantity for sauce. Vermont is a bastion of organic farming, and I can buy all the deformed beauties that I need. Some years, I grow eccentric varieties suitable for sauces and have cherry, beefsteak and at least two other kinds of tomatoes—perhaps a golden one—racing frost to ripeness. Other years, the selection is different. There are five kinds of basil to sit in the shade between the tomato rows.

While radishes are in every bed, in mine you will find only the French radish, small, round and red with a white tip, meant for eating with butter and salt as a first course. There are four kinds of hot peppers, but no bells; tiny oval Japanese egg-plants, round white ones and long, slim Chinese ones.

It's not harder to grow the round French string beans that are meant to be picked daily, slim and young (giving me an endlessly creaky back all summer), than the big, flat American beans. I also have a row of maroon-dappled pole beans for fresh eating, for freezing, and some to allow to get big and swollen so that the fall will be warmed by beans popped fresh from the pod.

Peas are standards since they lose their fresh-picked sweetness even more quickly than corn on the way from garden to stove. I plant two kinds, one for later-season eating and one early-ripening variety for the classicisms of a July Fourth feast with salmon. While I envy Thomas Jefferson his hundreds of varieties, this is all I can manage to keep staked—actually growing up branches that are stuck in the ground—and picked.

An insatiable salad eater, I grow odd let-tuces and chicories, Chinese and Japanese vegeta-bles, a wide variety of semihot and hot peppers, broccoli di rape, Savoy cabbage and anything else I cannot buy or use so much of that twice-a-day-trips out the door to the garden are easier than getting in the car for trips to the store.

I must admit to seeds smuggled illegally from France and Italy; there was the year of the ten varieties of radicchio. The large seed suppliers such as Burpee have gotten more adventurous; but a series of catalogues from specialists entice me more. Every part of the country has its own climate, and there are seedmen who specialize in plants for those areas. It is often easy to tell by the location of the company. I have begun to look at the catalogues of Canadian companies specializing in cold-climate growing.

There are also companies and barter groups that specialize in heritage seeds both from a desire to restore the production of disappearing species and to preserve a wide genetic basis for mutation.

I finish my planting with a variety of annuals to splash the garden with color and fill in the unplanted, or newly dead, bits of border. Many, the nasturtiums and calendulas for instance, will end up being eaten.

I can last out the wet time—mud season when the snow melts and the dirt roads rut—watching my egg boxes for the first small green leaves and dreaming of salad summers and near-vegetarian falls.

RITES OF SPRING

No matter how clear and crisp the days, how bright the sun glinting off the snow, I get tired of cold weather and lots of clothes. How glorious to welcome spring, to pack up wool scarves and boots, to stop making hearty soups and stews, and to start thinking about salads, picnics and cold soups. You can certainly tell I don't live in the sun belt. Even there, summer food is different from winter food. The warm climate turns to hot.

All over the world, and throughout history, spring has been a cause of celebration. Great religious holidays come in spring, with accompanying feasts that use the season's fresh herbs and vegetables, the first harvest of the year. Until recently, spring lamb was a featured dish in Western celebrations. But lately, for some odd reason, ham—really a fall and winter meat—has become part of the Easter celebration; and capon, part of Passover. I propose a return to lamb, especially since it is so readily, and inexpensively, available.

Lamb from Colorado ranks among America's best meats—fresh, mild and pale, rosy red in color. New Zealand lamb has a darker color and a deeper taste—more like European lamb—and is typically sold frozen. Look for the less widely available cuts of the younger, smaller, frozen lamb: a short leg will weigh four pounds, and four racks (two double racks) frozen together will serve only six people.

For the most springlike experience of all, order baby lamb—delicately flavored, very pale in color and best when served thoroughly cooked rather than rare. These baby lambs are tiny: A leg will weigh only two and one half to five pounds; a double rack of fourteen miniature chops weighs only a pound or two and will be meager fare for two. A whole baby lamb will feed only eight people. A perennial luxury, baby lamb does not come cheap.

In America, we eat less lamb than people do in most other countries. Perhaps what we need is to go back to simple, classic ways of cooking lamb—roasting and broiling—and then jazzing up the meal with some special accompaniments.

Worldwide, garlic is the top choice of seasoning for lamb, along with the fresh herbs of spring.

The arrival of spring also means the arrival of weeds. Thinking of them as potential delicacies may make cleaning up the lawn less painful. Small dandelion greens can go into your salad. Wild sorrel, with its small shield-shaped leaves, makes a soup that will send you out looking for sorrel even when you are not weeding.

For me, a sure sign of warm weather is the appearance of flowers—not exotic tropical or hothouse beauties—innocent, traditional blooms growing out of doors. An irrepressible cook, it immediately pops into my mind that many of them are not only beautiful and edible; but also that they taste good. In the past, I have omitted more than passing reference to edible flowers because florist-shop flowers cannot be used. Usually, they have been sprayed to discourage bugs. Unfortunately, that must also discourage the cook and the eater.

If you have a garden, it is worth taking a small section—part of the herb garden, for instance—and planting it with edible flowers. I guarantee that it will be beautiful and have color all season long. Plant the border with nasturtiums, not the dwarf kind, and marigolds. Just behind them put primroses, violets and pansies interspersed with various geraniums (true geraniums, delicate, small and pale in color, not those bright, gaudy house plants). The geraniums will fill in as the season for primroses and violas passes. Put in a few fragrant, old-fashioned roses. Add day lilies and tiger lilies toward the back, or the center if it's a bed that you walk around. Also in the back would go spider mums. The brilliant blue of anchusa, the darker blue of borage, the soft pink of mallows and the yellow of tansy are nice additions. This is, typically, a very old-fashioned, multicolored garden, part annual and part perennial. Kept close to a kitchen door, it is cheering and useful.

While I wouldn't put mints or their relatives such as marjoram in the edible flower garden—they are liable to overrun it—I would include pots of rosemary brought out from the house and a few clumps of chives that I would allow to flower. Zucchini and squash blossoms come from the vegetable garden along with dill flowers and the yellow flowers from overage mustard greens. Walks in fields produce wild flowers such as lemony-tasting pale pink bee balm, good to eat but a disorderly influence in the garden. The herb garden yields a wide variety of riches when some of it is allowed to bloom.

TOMATO TIMES

WHEN SUMMER FINALLY arrives, it may mean freckles, poison ivy and wet, sticky shirts. It also means no coats, the smell of damp when I weed after a summer storm, perfect berries and ripe vegetables. I love deep, dark Fairfax strawberries, tiny green beans, tart-sweet raspberries and, most of all, tomatoes of all shapes, sizes and colors.

I plant as many kinds as I have room for and buy what I don't. I have even come to be fond of tomato plants with their fuzzy leaves and the strange pungent perfume they give off in the hot summer sun. This smell at the stem end of a tomato—even in a store—is the sign of ripeness. It is acrid and tonic, but not at all sweet.

I plant plum tomatoes for sauce and paste, large beefsteaks, hoping that they will ripen before the frost, and cherry tomatoes, yellow and red. I have even located seed for the yet smaller, sweeter, round tomatoes that look like a bunch of grapes and that Italians dry in the sun upended on the plant as peppers are dried in the Southwest. Some thumbnail-size tomatoes can be tossed in salads—watch out, they spurt juice when you eat them—or they can be sautéed with olive oil, garlic and basil as a quick vegetable. I welcome the small, pear-shaped, shmoo-like red and yellow tomatoes that pop with juice as I crunch them in my mouth. I slice the golden yellow tomatoes—normal except for their sweetness and extra color. I even grow tomatilloes, husk tomatoes, for acid green sauces. Then I plant a quick-ripening tomato variety for first pleasure.

At summer's end, I pick and enjoy the remaining green tomatoes before the first frost turns them a hideous mushy black. I make pickles, relish and dip some slices in cornmeal and sear them quickly in a hot skillet just wiped with oil.

Sometimes I cheat, supplementing the seedlings that clutter bright windowsills before the soil is warm enough for planting with large, vigorous plants from a local nursery, which set fruit almost the minute they go into the ground. With a minimum of three kinds of basil in full leaf, a huge and vigorous lovage plant (worth seeking out and

154

planting where you have room for a large—six feet high and four feet wide—plant), dill, chives, summer savory, thyme and parsley, I am all set for summer-long self-indulgence.

In tomato season, the best fresh preparations are often the simplest. An emblematic tale is of Robert Courtine, one of the great French food writers. When he used to review restaurants, it was said he ordered a salade tomate as the first course no matter where he went, no matter how elegant the restaurant, feeling that it was a true test of a restaurant's devotion to good ingredients and proper technique.

The Italians approach great tomatoes informally but carefully. They don't add acid (lemon or vinegar), because they feel ripe tomatoes have enough. They cut the tomatoes about one quarter of an inch thick, overlap the slices and add only olive oil, basil, salt and pepper. The dressing that forms from the tomato juices and olive oil is then spooned on top. Italians use many different tomato varieties. Sometimes basil, shredded or in whole leaves, lends its tang. When tomatoes are combined with sweet onion and tiny, blanched green beans for one of the best summer salads, the red fruit is cut in wedges and lemon juice is added.

The French typically use small, even round tomatoes with bumpy shoulders. When they make salade tomate they peel the tomatoes first. A perfectly ripe tomato does not have to be dipped in simmering water before peeling. Run the back of the blade of a dinner knife over the entire tomato. Slip a sharp knife under the skin and pull. The skin will pull off. The tomatoes are sliced, sprinkled with salt, overlapped on a plate and topped with a vinaigrette. Recipes in nineteenth-century French cookbooks for the housewife do not call for peeling the tomato, but otherwise are identical to today's usage.

My salad varies only slight from the Italian version. I use thick red slices, salted and topped with chives, black pepper, very good olive oil and whole bush-basil leaves. If the tomatoes are very sweet, I may add a little lemon juice. I also spoon the juices.

When you add tomatoes to any salad, try salting them for a few minutes and then using the resulting liquid as part of the salad dressing. It will be less fattening.

You will note that salting and spooning does not give you ice-cold tomatoes. That is as should be. The appropriateness of room-warm tomatoes is also true of salsa cruda, which is nothing other than our friend the Italian tomato salad in chopped form. Sometimes chopped sweet onions or garlic is added. It is served over hot pasta.

The next level of complication is grilled slices of crusty bread brushed with garlicky oil and smothered with chopped tomatoes, onions and garlic—bruschetta.

Hot and semihot peppers ripen along with yellow tomatoes. Together they make a wonderful sauce for pasta when quickly sautéed in olive oil. Use one-half cup of good olive oil with twenty long, medium-hot peppers (gypsy peppers, for instance), eight cloves of thinly sliced garlic, six cups of ripe yellow tomatoes in wedges, and salt and pepper. While a pound of linguine is cooking, sauté the whole peppers for four minutes in hot oil; add garlic and tomatoes and continue to sauté for about five minutes. Pour over cooked pasta.

When tomatoes are cheap and mine are less than splendid, I buy a lot. They can be the imperfect, oddly shaped ones. I remember that the pink cardboard of winter tomatoes lies ahead. I spend time freezing, putting up and drying. Whole, perfect tomatoes can be frozen in individual freezer containers. Do not defrost tomatoes totally before using. Let them thaw just enough so that they can be cut up and cooked.

I make tomato purée and tomato paste to freeze—no salt or odd preservatives. Remove stem ends and any blemishes from your tomatoes. Cut them into chunks and cook on top of the stove, at low heat, stirring from time to time so that they do not scorch. When they are fully cooked, but still watery, put them through a food mill to remove the seeds and skin. Return to the stove and continue to cook, still over low heat, stir until enough evaporation has taken place and you have the consistency you want. The same thing can be more quickly done in a microwave oven.

Large, round American tomatoes will give a fresher-tasting, more acidic purée. Meaty Italian plum tomatoes will need much less cooking time—less water to evaporate—and will give a darker red, sweeter purée.

If labor is a proof of love, then the tomato is America's food of love. In a world in which gardening is the nation's largest outdoor activity, the tomato is the most widely homegrown and plentiful crop. It is also, if less obviously, our favorite flavor. Tomatoes are ubiquitous, so you may not notice that they pervade almost everything we eat. America's gift to world cooking shows up in foods Italian, Chinese and Thai, as well as in its native southern American home. It may be concealed by basil or coriander, hot peppers or garlic, fermented black beans or cream; but, just under the surface, there it is, America's favorite taste. It got ahold of us in childhood slathered on pizza, dripped onto hamburgers as ketchup, hugging pasta and helping salsas burn our mouths. Which is not to mention tomato juice, Bloody Mary mix and sun-dried tomatoes. Now it tops blue cornmeal pasta.

Tomatoes form the base of most of the sick-sweet commercial barbecue sauces noxious with tautological "liquid" smoke. Upscale, it marries with mozzarella to make insalata Caprese, a pernicious (because usually bad) sign of the times. By the by, where is all the buffalo milk mozzarella coming from? I've been to the south of Italy and only a few buffalo (water buffalo, not American Bison) were to be seen.

Steak houses are still serving slabs of so-called beefsteak tomatoes with accompanying tombstone-thick slices of onion under a sweet red dressing, once known as French.

The low point in the life of America's tomato must have been reached when the government, in its wisdom, decided that ketchup was a vegetable from the point of view of school lunch. For the record, one tablespoon of ketchup represents eighteen calories, 180 milligrams of salt and virtually no other nutrients, whereas a real-life, average tomato has twenty-four calories, only ten milligrams of sodium, and is loaded with potassium and vitamins.

Almost as low, but without the overt political implications—politico-economics is another tale—is the condition to which the supermarket tomato has been reduced by special breeding and early shipping for tomato appearance but wet, pink-cardboard taste in your mouth.

Into every void an expensive solution: Tomatoes are shipped from Holland and Israel and, down in Florida, they are trying to grow and trademark tomatoes that actually have some passing resemblance to the real thing. Out of season, canned tomatoes, tomato paste and jars of spaghetti sauce have been the cook's solution for many years.

If they are your solution, add some lemon juice to any preparation using them. The heat of cooking and packing robs these mixtures of the natural tomato acidity and you cannot taste sweet without acid.

Most tomato products are inexpensive. The better brands cost a little more than the average, but nothing our pockets cannot take. Watch out: All the prepared tomato products except for special dietetic brands are laden with salt.

If you want to start pretty much from scratch, but don't have great tomatoes or home-made purée on hand, then a good starting place is the purée in a sterile-pack carton put up in Italy. It is a kind of packaging Americans don't seem to take to easily any more than we have learned to use foods out of tubes although it is a current practice in Europe. I particularly like this way of purchasing tomato paste—otherwise, I am constantly stuck with nasty, blackening leftover bits in cans. The paste is better too, less sweet and fresher tasting.

If you feel a need for sun-dried tomatoes, you will find most of the ones that have been re-constituted are overpriced and not very good. If they are packed in olive oil, they are even more expensive and the oil isn't first rate. The best so-lution and the cheapest is to buy sun-dried tomatoes dry, heat them briefly in a little water and then, drained, in olive oil to cover and let them steep for one day or until you want to use them.

There are ways to have the taste of good tomatoes year round, but not by buying them in winter; summer and local are best for fresh.

NATURAL
COMBINATIONS

HAVE YOU EVER noticed how bizarre—
from the gardener's point of view (mine from
windy, late-spring, early-frost Vermont)—certain
standard combinations of foods in recipes are?
We need to take a second look at our recipes and
make judgments that only seasonal standards can
provide.

Nothing has been more automatic than peas
and carrots. Unless you are willing to pull the ti-
niest of carrot thinnings from the row—the kind
that should be sacrificed only to a gentle steaming
with a touch of butter—you have no carrots to go
with the peas when they are young and tender.
Only someone who uses vegetables that are not at

their best or who has become inured to vegetables from goodness knows where showing up in markets or on your plate at times that have nothing to do with local growing schedules can contemplate such pairings.

Lettuce and tomato obviously carry on a lunch-counter association. My lettuce has long bolted to seed and milky-sapped stalks before the tomatoes are ripe. How much more intelligently conceived is the Italian salad of blanched, tender string beans picked before they are two and one-half inches long with acid-ripe tomatoes and the first of the sweet onions. The old standby of tomatoes and cucumbers with dill and sour cream or yogurt instead of normal dressing also makes sense.

Yes, I put in a second crop of lettuce; but its tender leaves are not hardy enough to stand up to tomatoes. I serve the new leaves mixed with herbs and barely coated with a gentle dressing. The very late chicories—especially the radicchios—do best on their own or with the equally late bulb (Florence) fennel.

The Italian and Mexican combinations of tomatoes and peppers, hot and sweet, raw and cooked, take advantage of both vegetables in their prime; but watch out for avocado dishes that call for tomatoes—their perfections do not overlap.

The last of the asparagus may wait for the first of the spring peas, but not many of them.

That is why you will find them joined in risottos and garnishes where their precious scarcity is stretched and framed by bulkier ingredients.

Fresh corn and lima beans, which ripen at the same time, are normal as a combination in fresh succotash. A ratatouille that uses up every gardener's glorious, late-summer surplus of squashes, eggplants and tomatoes makes sense, but beware the inclusion of mushrooms. The best of late summer, the fresh porcini (cèpes, boletus), the trompette de la mort (black versions of chanterelles) and coral mushrooms, don't belong in stew.

Fruits invite the same distortions. Rhubarb and strawberries are a yes; strawberries and apples, no. My growing season is too short for melon; but if I could, I would know that only the second harvest of raspberries would yield fruit for mixing. Tiny huckleberries must live happily on their own with cream or in jam or pie. The early-ripening currants and gooseberries can be coupled with some sweet berries for summer pudding, but only for a brief ecstatic moment. Peaches can consort with raspberries and blackberries; but sweet cherries can dance only with apricots.

I suppose that town cooks with a supermarket glut of produce—not usually fully, naturally ripe—at every season from every part of the globe and those who come to vegetables with no more idea of fresh than what the freezer case provides should accept and create combinations that seem unnatural when standing in a burgeoning garden or at a midsummer farm stand.

I wonder who can test a cranberry and strawberry pie, or sorrel with midwinter fish. Spring sorrel has lovingly embraced spring shad and salmon for many years and should be left locked there, except for stellar appearances in cold and creamy soups or sauce for spring chicken. It would have to be very early spinach or antique potatoes from last year to join it in a purée.

Even in Turkey and Greece, figs are not ripe in August. They are the blessing of later sunny days. They can hardly grow where apples do. Best eaten raw, they should be left for cooking with the late-maturing quinces.

Fresh perennial herbs tend to blend with many things during their long seasons; but annuals like summer savory, dill and even basil do not really mature until the long, full-summer days. A biennial like parsley has been much abused by commercial growing and a sempiternal status as color, not flavor. A realization that garden parsley is a seasonal creature flourishing in August and on into the fall lets us use it with its best friends and leave the peas to the early, invasive mints, the string beans to the just-ready savory and sage. Asparagus can go with dill only in supermarket cuisine.

Even the eruption of flowers bestrewing every dish in town should observe the normal blooming times and careful avoidance of any bush or plant that has been sprayed. The bright red sage can go with cucumbers, but not with the earliest spring greens. A Monet-like rainbow of nasturtiums can go with genuine veal—not those huge beasts with artfully, but unfortunately, white flesh. Tea-rose petals can be candied for peaches; but violets won't wait beyond the first wild strawberries. Chive blossoms bereft of their tough mooring are a lavender sprinkle for the first spinach and lobster, but not for cold-weather clams and oysters. Calendulas wait for the first of the winter squash.

The merit of paying attention to the natural order of growth is to have food that is local, naturally ripe and flavorful. It also restores the delight of novelty with each season, each week of summer, bringing a new arrival, fleeting enough to be cherished and made much of. It is seasonal exuberance and plenty that inspire the cook to innovation, the new variation on a theme without any cloying of the ingredient. The raw tomato salad and the three hundreth variation on tomato sauce are equally enjoyable.

However, natural succulence will limit the tendency to overcook, overseason, oversalt and oversauce. Long live fresh.

SPOILED

WHEN ROSES—IF not calla lilies—are in bloom and we can find or pick wonderful, local tomatoes, it may be a relatively unpainful time to reflect on the fact that we are spoiled—not by the glories of the season, but by our childlike unwillingness to accept limitation in any season. It used to be grand dukes and madmen who ate strawberries in December. One had to be a very wealthy person indeed to maintain succession houses (greenhouses of various temperatures) that would provide grapes for midwinter invalids. No one expected tomatoes in January.

Today, we demand tomatoes all year around, get out-of-season fruits from South America and New Zealand and then complain about the quality and pesticides used in countries we cannot control.

Even midsummer, we look for unblemished fruits and vegetables, ignoring the hard reality that these seeming glories, like Snow White's apple, may be poisoned—poisoned with just those sprays we say we want to avoid.

The only way that we are going to get better food is to control ourselves, to accept limitation. We must cease buying pink cardboard in winter. In summer, we must search out organic fruits and vegetables, ignoring their flaws in honor of their healthfulness and often better flavor. We may even have to pay more.

We will certainly have to pay more for organic, free-range chickens and eggs. By doing so we will avoid hormones, have eggs with yolks of a brighter gold verging on orange, and with flavor. We will gain chickens with more taste and will have a better chance of avoiding salmonella infection.

It is a tragedy that in such a rich country we have to be deeply concerned with the safety and quality of our basic products. Why should we eat beef that is unacceptable for sale in the United Kingdom due to hormones? We have gotten into this fix because we want bigger and cheaper. Instead, we must concern ourselves with lobbying and political action. We must set standards, cease polluting our waters and soil, have government inspection.

I would rather take a conscious risk like the Japanese do in eating fugu than take unconscious risks all the time with everyday foods. Each consumer must decide what is an acceptable risk: whether to swallow clams? Even then, we have a right to know that that seafood comes from inspected waters.

I find it unacceptable that there are classic recipes that I cannot safely make, serve and write about. The salmonella-in-the-egg problem prohibits mayonnaise, mousse, poached eggs, egg-white-lightened sorbets, egg-yolk-rich ice creams, meringues and egg-bound sauces. None of these get hot enough to sterilize the eggs.

Some health hazards can be taken care of with proper food preparation. We can cook our chickens and our fish to a high enough temperature for a long enough time to kill harmful bacteria and parasites. We cannot cook an oyster long enough and still have it be edible.

Yes, the food supply is probably safer than it was in prerefrigeration times; but with societal affluence comes choice, and we do not have to accept the unsafe out of hungry desperation. We almost eliminated tuberculosis and listeria-infected milk from our lives generations ago. It is time to remove other hazards both old—salmonella—and new—pesticides.

Perhaps if we return to seasonal foods and decide that good, clean food is worth searching out and paying for, we will even value and enjoy it more. It will certainly taste better.

Speaking of taste, I must offer a few rewards for putting up with unpleasant reality and as an encouragement for accepting virtuous self-limitation. Safe sex isn't the only self-control we need practice.

If we encourage sustainable agriculture and local, small-scale farming, we will find a greater variety of foods available to us. Enormous farms have to plant crops that are in general enough demand to warrant planting in hundred-acre tracts. A small farmer or orchardist may be able to offer the tiny, yellow, French mirabelle plums, white peaches and mulberries that travel poorly but have unequaled perfume and flavor on their own or in lightly sweetened preserves.

White peaches are the right kind, incidentally, for a Bellini. Simply purée the fruit in a blender or food processor with just enough lemon juice to prevent discoloration. Put through a fine sieve. Refrigerate until very cold. Fill a Champagne flute halfway with your peach syrup, and, stirring with a long spoon (otherwise it froths too much), fill the rest of the way with cold Prosecco or another dry bubbly. The peach syrup freezes really well. That's the proper way to have your peaches in January.

Similarly, the inexpensive plentitude of ripe plum tomatoes can be made into a freezable purée. We can look for varieties of tomatoes that are deemed by the promotion-minded too ugly for sale, too perishable for shipping, and so rescue real beefsteak tomatoes from "progress," "improvement" and extinction.

Even without the gain of inexpensive produce for putting-up, there are advantages in supporting and knowing local growers. We may be able to convince farmers that there is sufficient reward in digging potatoes when they are so tiny that they merely need to be wiped with a damp cloth—scrubbing will remove their tender skins— and steamed in a little butter.

Orchardists who care enough to grow unsprayed apples are often those who preserve older varieties—there used to be hundreds on the market—that make a better pie, such as russets, reinettes and pippins. We will make our baked apples with Rome Beauties. We may even find orchards that grow quinces, permitting us to try a whole new set of recipes and avoid the pectin that has replaced quince as a gelling factor.

While we consider ways of preserving older virtues and current produce, we should be aware of our too-ready use of plastics. Containers and wraps should be reusable or we are contributing in

another way to the destruction of our environment.

It all requires a little more work, a little more money; but the rewards, in addition to flavor, are a healthier us, healthier children and a healthier society with fewer long-term medical costs.

ENJOYING
GUESTS

POLITE TODAY: ETIQUETTE FOR THE NEW DINNER PARTY

THERE WAS A time, and not so long ago either, that no well-brought-up girl (we weren't women then) would be seen out of doors without gloves. In appropriately warm weather or on formal evenings, the gloves were white and preferably made of the thinnest kidskin. This led to special frames for drying the gloves after they had been washed and wooden glove stretchers to use before the gloves went on for the first time or after they were washed. This was necessary since the gloves were supposed to fit wrinkleless, as tight as a second skin. In turn, there was a whole set of questions with rules for answers: For whom did one ease off the gloves before shaking hands? what did one do in the improbable event that some European gentleman wanted to kiss one's hand? what happened to the gloves come dinnertime?

Gloves have disappeared except as a fashionable whimsy or extravagance, and the elaborate dinner party etiquette that went with them has dwindled into invisibility as well. Indeed, in recent years I have felt rather irrelevant because I insisted on writing about home entertaining. Now, with one more twist of the mores, it turns out that people are having people into their homes for dinner once again.

It is not the same kind of entertaining that went on when I was a child or even when I was a young married. Then I felt the need for formality, for doing it right, and right meant pomp and days of cooking. Today, neither I nor anyone else has all that time. Short of weddings and proms, few people are summoned anywhere by formal cards of invitation demanding a formal, written response. I have recently noticed that experienced hostesses who invite a good deal ahead of time for largish parties have taken to sending out reminder cards, a sign not so much of our formality as our bad manners.

There was a time when a party meant getting help, someone to clean up and even someone to help serve. While it is a ravishing notion, it is a highly improbable one. Your guests will just have to accept the fact that you are the help. At a seated dinner, I tell them firmly to stay seated, I don't want anyone seeing the mess in my kitchen. If you are comfortable with help from your guests, accept it. Try to arrange things so that no more than one guest or a previously designated close friend gets up at each course. Otherwise, everybody feels they ought to get up, and the party falls apart. If you are going to have professional servers, get enough of them. It is annoying for some people to wait while their food is getting cold because others haven't been served.

Remember, even Emily Post allowed people to start eating as soon as four people had been served. If you are the hostess and you have a well-raised Southern boy at the table, please pick up your fork and eat. Otherwise, he'll sit there, starving, waiting for you to begin.

When I was first married, I remember with some fondness that giving a dinner party meant ironing a fragile tablecloth, getting out the seldom-used silver flatware and polishing it, carefully washing crystal stemware in boiling hot water and drying it with a linen towel, buying candles, arranging flowers and setting everything out in the studied order prescribed by Victorian custom. Forks went to the left of the plate in order of use, moving from the farthest from the plate toward the plate. Knives and spoons went to the right in the same order. That is, unless the fork and spoon were for dessert, in which case they went at the top of the plate.

The end of dinner meant washing everything and putting it away for another year. There was a reward though: Guests sent flowers. Sending them before the event was politer since it was not so much a quid pro quo for what had been received but rather a grace note of grateful anticipation. Flowers were generally sent prearranged, so that the hostess would not be subjected to a last-minute search for a vase. Today, if flowers come at all, they are usually in the hand of the arriving guest.

I was capable of using four or five forks (fish course, main course, salad and dessert, and even an oyster fork), three spoons (soup, dessert and coffee), and four knives (butter, fish, meat and cheese). The glasses multiplied with the wines. Between salad and dessert, I put finger bowls on plates lined with cloth doilies and floated a slice of lemon or a rose petal on the barely warm water. I put place cards in front of each setting and ashtrays and little glass holders for cigarettes at every other place—it was a different world. Before my time, but barely, there were nut dishes to be set before each place after dessert and footed stands with fruit, grape shears and nut picks to be set in the center of the table at the same time.

All that was without even cooking the food.

In those days, china came in sets—twelve of each thing—and everything matched. Time's attrition has left me with few even twelves.

From time to time, I still make the gala effort and enjoy the pomp and beauty. Today, however, I am unwilling to let all that fuss and formality inhibit my ability to entertain. I just don't have the time, and, frankly, I find that not all guests are comfortable in such ornate settings. I don't want more attention placed on the party than on the guests. The world has changed and so have I.

By the by, if there are more than eight people, place cards are still not a bad idea. It saves that awkward moment when, peering at the list and pointing with a finger, you try to get milling guests seated. If you have a guest of honor, he or she usually belongs next to the hostess or host; but after that, seating patterns are a lot looser than once they were. People no longer come in neat pairs with one person of each sex. It is no disaster to have more women than men or vice versa. While six and ten people can alternate man/woman, with a man and a woman conventionally placed at either end of the table, that fact should no longer determine your guest list. The number of chairs is a much more relevant deciding factor.

My attitude toward my good things has changed also. I found out that silver didn't need polishing if it was used all the time and it was durable; it doesn't wear away with use. China need not match. I buy plates as I find them and like them. If I find five, I buy them. There are many nights when four is just the right number for dinner. I enjoy changing plates—from pattern to pattern—between courses. It livens up the table. I tend to avoid any plate with gold or silver trim; everything has to go into the dishwasher.

That holds for my stemware. While I like the edge at the lip to be thin; I won't buy anything anymore so fragile or expensive that I am uncomfortable putting it in the dishwasher. As food has changed, our table settings and even manners have changed along with it. Pasta doesn't require the same equipment as a steak, and more of us are enjoying pasta than red meat these days.

The rules for wine used to be rather ornate at formal dinners—Champagne before dinner, Sherry with the soup, white wine with the fish, Bordeaux with the meat, Burgundy with the cheese and a sweet wine with dessert. Even at less formal meals, there was the notion of white with fish and chicken, red with meat. Today, as I eat more fish and chicken but prefer red wine, I tend to serve red wine no matter what I am eating. If I want a truly fabulous bottle of red and I'm not having red meat, I add some cheese and drink the wine with that. Italian wine can go with American food and American wine with French food. There are fewer pieties, and it is up to us to taste and decide what will make a good combination.

Today's dishes may be attractive, permanent plastic, homey earthenware, spatter-dashed enamel or oriental lacquer. They won't be paper or flimsy plastic, I hate the spills and the leaks. Besides, the tableware should look deliberate and attractive. The glasses may be handsomely clunky tumblers rather than stemware. Flatware can be good-looking stainless steel, even the inexpensive French café stuff with the colored handles (unless it has been discolored by the dishwasher) or permanent chopsticks rather than the paper-wrapped come-with-the-order kind.

A recent purchase was a group of large, round plastic trays with low rims to use instead of placemats. They make it easy to clean up and protect the wooden table. I used to use an elegant place or service plate—no more. It's another dish to clean up, and usually one sufficiently fragile that it requires hand washing. I have come to like the look of a bare table that is clean and polished, if relevant. That happily rules out tablecloths, which now remain neatly folded in a drawer. If the day ever comes when I want to be more formal again, I may find that I have the cloths but no napkins, since I use the napkins all the time.

When I feel the need for a cloth, say at a buffet party when I suddenly have odd rented tables to cover, it is easy to buy inexpensive but cheerful yard goods and cut them in lengths with a pinking shears.

I tend to draw the line at paper napkins except at cocktail parties. A few years ago, I found some terrific, loosely woven French napkins that really don't need any ironing. The standard no-iron napkins always looked wrinkled to me. However, large paper napkins in bright, clear colors can look as if you meant it instead of looking like a mistake.

There is still the problem about where on the set table to place the napkin. If you can count on your guests to put the napkin on their laps immediately, you can place the napkin smack dab in front of them. Otherwise, it should go to the left of the fork, which can make for space problems, especially as I tend to collect large white napkins in junk shops. I really don't care whose initials they are sporting. They are big and the fabric is wonderful. It is often convenient to roll a place setting's worth of silver in a napkin for each person at a buffet meal so that people don't have to go to different piles, trying to remember what to pick, forgetting something and having to break into the line. If you serve something messy like mussels or lobster in the shell, count on an extra napkin per person. I have taken to passing out large paper napkins at this point to supplement the cloth ones and to avoid good napkins that smell fishy.

For many of us without dining rooms or even dining tables, the real problem may be where to eat. I have—in my youth—spread fabric or a large blanket topped with a sheet on the floor and had picnics there. No stem glasses and informal food—a pot of pasta, a salad, bread and cheese, and red wine was an ideal menu (cheap, quick, and it called for only two burners)—were appropriate. Card tables and folding chairs make a short-time solution. Using the stove as buffet table is do-able. If there is really no space, plates of finger foods, from spareribs to chicken wings, can be set around the room. Remember to have large bowls available for the bones as well as piles of paper napkins strategically placed for the fingers.

Cocktail parties require the least food and the least space for food. Buffet parties are the next most efficient. Attractive cooking pots can hold the food. I wouldn't use stainless-steel bowls, but china mixing bowls or clean-colored plastics can work. You don't need an array of silver. If you want silver, it can be rented and then you don't have to wash it. Today, almost anything can be rented, including the guests. If you have invited your grandmother, it is kind to make sure that she has a chair, even at a buffet party, and that it is next to a table where she can put her food, or provide one of those little folding tables.

Buffet food should come in small pieces that do not require a knife. It is hard enough to manage a plate, a glass and a fork if standing or sitting on a squishy chair or on the floor.

If I'm having a sit-down dinner, I often serve the food family style—much easier on a host without help. I set up a little table near the dining room table (not in a dining room) and put all the dishes and serving spoons and stuff I will need for the meal there. If I start with cold food, say smoked salmon, I have it already on plates at people's places when they come in. I bring in the main course to the serving table and dish it out from there. Later I serve salad and even dessert from there.

The easiest new meal may be take-out Chinese. While I have happily eaten from white cardboard containers, that seems a little informal for guests other than one's children. Fortunately, Chinese food can be put out in a few attractive bowls that need not match, although they should look as if they have a nodding familiarity. Each guest should get a good-sized rice bowl to heap with each food in turn. If you're serving tea, that will require another cup—preferably handleless—and soup will use yet a third. Chopsticks will take care of everything for those who can use them; a few sympathy forks on the table might be kind. If you buy soup, remember soup spoons.

Even this simple meal can have grace notes. Chopstick rests preclude messy tables. Inexpensive, Asian saucers can be bought and the nasty little packages of soy and mustard or duck sauce can be squeezed out into them for each person. If you are having beer, a glass may not be necessary; but it does make things look a bit less impromptu.

I guess that is the secret of the new hospitality and the way in which it stems from the old etiquette. Guests should feel that you truly want them to be there, that some planning and intention has gone into the evening, and that you care that they are comfortable and that the table looks attractive.

This, as you can see, doesn't mean that endless cooking must go on. We can emulate the French, who have been buying pâté as a first course and a tart for dessert for years. Even salad greens can now be bought all washed from a salad bar. That leaves you with only a main course to make, and that can be as simple as grilled marinated fish along with some spicy rice, which can be made ahead. With a good take-out food store, even the main course need not be cooked. A few roast chickens on a platter and a prepared vegetable, such as ratatouille in a bowl, can look sufficiently festive. It's a particularly good way to entertain at the last minute.

While I love last-minute invitations for casual get-togethers, if it is to be a real party, invitations should go out as much as a month and not less than two weeks before the day. It is a good idea to give guests some idea of the level of formality you are planning, since dinner can mean almost anything these days. While you may seldom need to say, "it's a black tie evening," you may want to say, "it will be very informal," or "we're having a few people over to celebrate such and such," or "we'll be watching the game and having something simple to eat." These tell guests how to dress and what to expect.

It is still polite for guests to arrive on time, but not early when I haven't quite finished dressing. Fifteen minutes late is about the maximum allowable. If some guests are very rude and arrive more than a half to three-quarters of an hour late, do not keep everybody waiting to eat. They will get cranky, maybe drink too much, and you will end up with dishes at three in the morning.

Even in the new, more casual etiquette, it is important for guests and hosts to observe some minimum ground rules if everything is to go well. Everything is possible as long as there is some consideration.

SIMPLE SETTINGS

MANY PEOPLE HAVE barely entertained in years, or have never entertained. They worked and felt they didn't have time to cook or didn't know how. The whole apparatus of party giving was forbidding. Sometimes we must entertain whether we want to or not. Some of us are beginning to think of party giving as a happy idea; but unfamiliarity breeds fear. Will the party work? Will the food be good enough? Just how do I do it? As an answer and to banish trepidation, I recommend simplicity and a strict antisnob attitude. I have never known anybody to complain about a home dinner because there weren't any butlers or because the meal was simple, as long as it was ample and good. People are delighted to be welcomed into a loving home; no one has to show off.

In recent years, it seems to me that there has been too much stress on complicated recipes and expensive or hard-to-find ingredients. I must say my mea culpas along with the rest of the food writers. What is needed today is more recipes that are relatively inexpensive, not recherché, and that do not make too many demands on rusty cooking skills. Nowhere is it written that expensive, fancy and hard equal good. They may or they may not. Simple, direct and flavorful can often be very good.

The thing to do is to choose a menu that seems reasonably simple and reasonably inexpensive particularly when it feeds a crowd. Do ahead what can be done ahead, including setting up the table.

The important thing is to do only as much as is comfortable for you, or you will make your guests tense. If possible, allow yourself twenty minutes of doing nothing before the guests arrive.

THEY WON'T EAT IT

When I was a child, I was haunted by the clean-plate club with its endless injunctions to "eat it all up," sometimes softened by the happy bunny whose picture on the bottom of the dish one was supposed to reveal by approved gluttony. There were appeals to sad thoughts of far-distant starving children: Chinese, Armenian or American Indian. (Fill in the disaster of your era.) The same world enforced "no dessert until you finish all your vegetables." I was left from adolescence onward with the struggle against being overweight and a horror of the words "healthy" and "robust." I knew they were polite ways of saying chubby.

Happily gone with the encouragement to

omnivorousness is the necessity of eating until stuffed and of eating soggy, smelly Brussels sprouts. Oddly, I find that there are some manners of that time for which I have a certain nostalgia. Guests trained as I was do not turn to the hostess and say flatly, even proudly: "I don't eat that." Manners were manners. Everybody was supposed to accommodate to all sorts of foods no matter how icky the tastes of the host might be, which led to haunting stories of diplomats being given the eye of the sheep as a sign of honor or being invited to a banquet where the pièce de résistance was dog.

Today, we live in a more self-oriented world. Each person seems to have his own particular diet, which is equated with a notion of salvation whose intensity does not seem entirely secular. There are vegetarians—even vegans, the followers of religions that prohibit the ingestion of pork, nonscaly fish or beef, Pritikin followers, diabetics, gall-bladder sufferers, no-red-meat eaters, a few die-hard macrobioticists, cholesterol watchers, your run-of-the-mill weight loss person, your food phobic, and people who suffer from a seemingly endless array of food allergies, from the tiny seeds in raspberries to wheat, milk and seafood, through to the exotica of every meat except things that grow in the wild. There is also the recovering alcoholic.

Epidemically, salt is avoided without any sense of whether such avoidance is a real medical obligation; but it is safer to assume that when people say they are on a low- or no-salt diet that they mean it.

Added to this is the current version of sheep's eyes: the loathing. This means that rabbits, eels, kidneys, liver (unless heavily disguised as pâté), kidneys, Bambi (otherwise known as venison), and anything slimy such as tripe or tapioca had best be omitted from the dinner party menu. It is well to keep in mind that many otherwise reasonable people are squeamish about fish with bones, and that some are uncomfortable eating with their hands.

It is no wonder that as a hostess I long a little for a time when people felt compelled to eat what was set before them. I am not heartless; I don't want my guests to be ill; but sometimes coming up with a menu that will satisfy everybody seems impossible.

As a hostess, I find the forthright approach best. It is unpleasant to be in medias res of proud service when confronted with rejection of labor-intensive food and the need to go out and whip up an omelet so the poor invitee has something to eat—unless, of course, the guest is allergic to eggs.

It has gotten to the point where if I am inviting people to my house for the first time I ask them if there is anything they don't eat. After the first time, it is my job to remember. I don't make bloody-red rib roast—even if I can afford it—when a vegetarian friend is coming to dine. Conversely, if someone is on an extremely restricted diet, say the yogi who is out on leave from the ashram, I will make sure there is something he can eat— brown rice can be served with almost any meal— but I don't make all the guests suffer for one self-depriver. I serve other foods as well. This provides what I hope will be the ample compensation of superiority to the abstainer.

There are guests who use their eating patterns as a club with which to attack the hostess. I find it hard to forget the guest who quite properly advised me that she was on a severely restricted gall-bladder diet. I happily steamed a whole, lean fish, provided bread without fat and served up a scrumptious sauce for the non-dieters. She sat stonily refusing to eat a morsel. This is the same woman who, at her own home, served lavish spreads and insisted that everybody eat beyond the realm of comfort. There was also the notable evening when an old friend brought his new wife to dine. She was what I, many years later, can define as an anorectic. She refused to eat anything but a boiled egg. Happily, they are divorced, and the current wife loves to eat. People like that don't get invited again.

The problem posed, what are the solutions? The recovering alcoholic is a relatively benign problem. Just don't push the wine. Have water glasses at every place and put attractive decanters with water around the table. If you have someone to help you serve, alert them to the fact that a certain person should not have wine poured. That way your guest is not in the position of having to say no all the time. An essential rule of entertaining is not to make the guest conspicuous. It is essential not to serve dishes with uncooked wine or spirits in them, such as zabaglione. I tend to avoid any wine- or liquor-flavored dish as well—too evocative and panic-making.

Before dinner, it's a good idea to have fruit juices and sodas available—not just for the recovering alcoholic. People are drinking less in general, and they often do this by saving their alcohol for dinner. I do have one friend who insists on watering even the best wine; I avert my eyes.

By the by, some people feel they cannot tolerate red wine; the tannin gives them a headache. I always keep an emergency bottle or two of white in the fridge.

I have a friend who claims to be able to drink only Chianti. He tends to suffer migraine headaches, and his doctor told him that Chianti contains no migraine-inducing histamines. He says it works, and I serve Chianti with pleasure. The problem is somewhat more complicated than he thinks. Histamine is a normal by-product of wine making. While there is an Italian scientific paper that says Chianti has no histamines, more recent research seems not to bear this out. It is true that wines that do not throw a malolactic, secondary, fermentation are lower in histamines. Young wines also are somewhat lighter in histamines and northern Italian reds are lower than Burgundies. The lowest of all seem to be the Champagnes.

Wine labels are no help in helping friends who declare themselves sensitive to sulfites, although they must realize that they occur in all fruits and vegetables and that store-bought orange juice has many. Since wine labels must now say that the wine contains sulfites if it has more than 10 parts per million—a minuscule amount; the legal limit in America is under 30 parts per million—almost all wine makers and/or importers now put the containing-sulfites label on the bottle no matter how much sulfite the wine actually contains.

Sulfur is added to a wine to promote cleanliness. Champagne makers try to minimize sulfur, since the bubbles carry any slightly off odor quickly to the nose. There are some wine makers who are following more rigorous cleanliness measures to minimize or eliminate the use of sulfur. These wines may be hard to find, and it will require extensive conversation with a knowledgeable wine merchant.

The guests on salt-free diets can be dealt with by a clever cook. Ethnic dishes such as Moroccan fish tagines, Mexican chicken mole or Moghul braised dishes (korma or dompuckht) are always good, as the high seasoning levels mask the lack of salt. In other kinds of cooking, up the spice levels; add extra acid—lemon juice, good vinegar, red peppers, good tomatoes or tomatillos—and brandish handfuls of fresh herbs. Be careful about using canned ingredients such as stock, tomatoes, and premade sauces and seasoning mixtures. They are liable to be high in salt. It's no fair cheating with soy sauce. Since many of the salt-free eaters are also the butter, red meat and cholesterol avoiders, head for the olive oil and the fish (not seafood).

I have a small collection of glass plates. This permits me to serve the truly kosher. I buy a single portion of fish that in nature had both scales and gills and I put it on the plate with some neatly sliced vegetables. I season and cover it with plastic wrap. Just as everybody is sitting down, I put the plate in the microwave oven for a few minutes and serve forth with some lemon. I keep place settings of uncontaminated (used only for these guests) silver.

Vegetarians provide lesser problems even if they are vegans. If they are very strict, serve them kosher wines—no egg, animal or milk products are used in the fining. Do find out what kind of vegetarians these guests are, however. A carefully prepared meal of vegetarian lasagna can be ruined for just the guests you were particularly trying to please by the Béchamel and the cheese. Two standbys of mine are a vegetarian couscous and a vegetarian feijoada. The whole crowd can eat happily without knowing the meal is vegetarian. These foods tend to be good for the no-salt, no-red-meat crowd as well. Salad and cheese add the relaxation of an extra course plus a little animal protein and calcium, at least for the other guests and for the vegetarians if they're not vegans. If in doubt, put the cheese on a separate plate so as not to sully the salads of the pure. Dessert can be extravagant; but have some berries or melon on hand for the strict and lean.

Incidentally, we also entertain in restaurants. It is almost impossible to so entertain the kosher. It may be almost as hard to find a restaurant for a vegetarian. Italian ones, what with pasta and lots of vegetable dishes and the uses of olive oil rather than butter, are the easiest; but you may want to check with the restaurant you have chosen before you go. Other kinds of eaters can usually find something on a reasonably diverse menu.

Even if the strict and lean are not vegetarians and don't think of themselves as odd in any way, they probably recoil these days at the sight of blood and fat. A whole large poached fish is probably the safest solution, although I enjoy the homeliness of two perfectly roasted and herb-stuffed chickens. The chickens require that you know how to carve, and the fish that you are comfortable with filleting. A stir-fry of skinned and boned chicken or shrimp with lots of fresh vegetables should offend no one, please everybody and not embarrass you.

Food for guests with allergies is easy; avoid the offending ingredients. This may be easier said than done if milk and wheat are the problems. Potatoes or rice instead of bread solve the main-course starch; but dessert may be more difficult. Angel food cake is ideal unless there is an egg problem, although the allergy is most often to egg yolks, which permits angel food, perhaps with a strawberry sauce. If no eggs can be eaten, go back to poached fruit, which can be served with a fruit sauce.

Diabetics are easy to please. Do not serve dishes with sugar and keep the starches on the side so that these guests can make their own decisions about how much they are allowed. It is also better to keep the fat reduced to a minimum.

Develop a little repertoire of low-fat, low-salt cheeses so that you can proudly serve a cheese course to almost anybody. Many of these cheeses were first developed in Europe for health-conscious, cheese-loving Europeans. They are excellent and now some good ones are made in America. Fromage blanc is another perfect answer to the problem. Serve with berries and pass bowls of crème fraîche and sugar for the self-indulgent.

All of this leaves me with a select guest list of friends who will eat anything; try any wine. In fact, they enjoy it. I cherish them so that I can indulge all my culinary pleasures and know that they will help create a good time. Watch out, however, for unknown dates.

The Guest's Side

I myself can be the problem guest. I cannot eat crab. I have a truly dreadful allergic reaction guaranteed to stop any dinner party dead in its tracks, since I swell up, turn red and cease to breathe. Hostesses and waiters who lie to the allergic—"No, there's no crab in this fish soup"— ought to be shot. After several distressing incidents in San Francisco, where cooks have proudly presented me with the well-intentioned luxury of a seasonal crab feast, I have learned to say, apologetically, when invited for dinner: "I'm sorry but I don't eat crab." If the invitation is to a Baltimore blue-crab boil, I turn it down with explanations; but if it's for a normal dinner party, I figure the cook has time to adapt.

As a guest, it is better to mention one's gastronomic peculiarities when invited. It saves embarrassment all around. If you are severely diabetic or on an extremely restricted ulcer diet—nothing but pablum—it is kind to say you would love to come, but there is this problem and you will understand perfectly if another evening is better or that you can just come by for drinks and coffee. Then it is up to the host.

It is not acceptable to ask what is being served any more than it is to ask who the guests will be. If you think your ex-spouse might be invited and the inviter is a friend, you can say: "By the way, I'm not comfortable being at a party with Max." If it's a bigger or more formal event, try to behave like an adult. Then you can decide if the hostess is dumb or mischievous. Having stated your minimum objections to a meal, let it go.

If you cannot drink, just ask for some water instead. If pushed, you can say simply: "I'm not drinking these days." This is not the time for your life story.

If it's simply a question of a real distaste for something, follow the old rule: Eat a little and, if asked tactlessly if you don't like it, say that, depending on the place in the meal, either that what came before was so delicious you filled up, or that you are saving yourself for the rest of the meal. A pointer to hosts: Don't ask.

If you find yourself at a dinner, as the guest of a guest, where you haven't had a chance to warn the cook about your dietary restrictions and you are served something you cannot eat, say so; but say it calmly, firmly and apologetically unless it is at a large dinner where no one will notice that you are not eating. If the hosts offer an alternative, say it's not necessary but kind, and if it's really not too much trouble, that would be fine when they get a chance. Be prepared to wait. There are other diners whose meals shouldn't be ruined.

Try not to imply when refusing meat, salt or a luscious dessert that you are either a finer or more elegant person than the other guests, or that what they are eating is vaguely or overtly disgusting. Let's hope for the hostess's sake that they will enjoy their dinner. From the point of view of being a guest, even if you deeply believe that killing animals is criminal, now is not the time to say it. Just don't eat the meat.

Once again, to avoid all such sticky nuances, tell the host or hostess what you cannot (will not) eat. If invited to the dinner by a friend other than the hosts, try to get the friend to convey the message.

If the hosts are rude enough to push you, i.e., "Just have a sip of the wine," try saying, "No thank you" before actually barking; but if they are rude to the extreme, you may not have any choice.

"THE ROCKETS' RED GLARE"

THE FOURTH OF July is the most American of holidays. It is time to bring it back, not with hoopla and commercialism, but with more than a moment's pause for old-fashioned sentiments of love and appreciation for our country and its values, to see it as more than a day off.

Thanksgiving is ours, also, but is linked to international harvest festivals. Martin Luther King's birthday and that strange, compound birthday, Presidents' Day, are significant; but it seems to me that the birthday of our country calls most positively to most of us.

From the ideals of democracy, it may seem like an abrupt leap to food; but to me, celebrations

mean food and the Glorious Fourth has traditionally been a time for families and feasts, community
parades and church suppers, with veterans of a variety of wars marching proudly.

Sometimes, all the talk of recent years about
trendy and regional American food has made me
feel uneasy; but the foods I think of for our prime
summer holiday seem comfortable, uncontrived,
American and right. They come from a hodge-
podge of heritages and our own plentiful ingredients, and have been enjoyed so often, their recipes
adopted and adapted by so many cooks that they
have truly become our own.

The abundance of ingredients can most
quickly be understood if we look at our celebratory
whole hams and whole salmons. Typically, in Europe, these are great delicacies, smoked or cured
and then served in the thinnest possible slices. For
many years, when I had friends visiting from
abroad, I would impress them by serving a whole
baked ham. To them it seemed profligate.

For the Fourth, the simplest and best main
event is a whole salmon—pale and elegantly Atlantic or bright red, rich and sockeye Pacific—
poached in anything from a long, skinny and fancy
French pot to the oven, the dishwasher or my favorite, the microwave oven. Tenderly removed
from its cooking container, foil, or cloth and laid in
splendor on a large platter, it is the center of the
feast.

The simplest rule for cooking fish any way but in the microwave is the old Canadian cooking method. Measure the fish at its thickest part. Allow ten minutes' cooking time for each inch of thickness and a fraction of the ten minutes for fractions of inches. For instance, a fish that measures three and one-half inches will need to cook for thirty-five minutes.

If you are serving the fish cool—at room temperature, not gelid—lift the skin off the fish when it's still warm from the pot. After the fish cools, the skin sticks like glue. If a whitish bloom appears on the pink flesh as it cools, scrape it gently with the back of a knife and off it comes. If the first true watercress is flourishing in our streams, a layer of it can be a bed for the fish served cold.

Lemons, yes, but sauces—even mayonnaise, tartar, or Hollandaise if the fish is hot—aren't needed. There will be mayonnaise-rich potato salad with hard-boiled eggs and pimientoes, coleslaw and, best of all, new peas rushed from the vines to be simmered briefly and just coated with a little sweet butter and maybe a hint of the first mint.

To be honest, my favorite potato salad is not made with homemade mayonnaise. It uses the particularly American stuff straight out of the jar. I love German potato salad and French potato salad and all sorts of fancier versions; but my favorite true-blue potato salad would be unrecognizable without the commercial product.

If the coasts with cold-water rivers are too far, crab or shrimp may be boiled up in big pots of spicy water or beer, or fried chicken may rule the roost. The go-withs will stay the same.

The perfect ending is strawberry shortcake with rich, dark seasonal berries barely rinsed, carefully hulled, sliced and tossed with just a hint of sugar. The hulling is critical. Too often, even in the almost best restaurants, the ends of strawberries are simply sliced off—wrong! One needs to take a very sharp, small knife and make a conical cut around the stem, removing stem and lighter-colored inner pith in one go. The difference in flavor and texture is splendid. The only time strawberries should be left unhulled is when they are piled into a dish stems on. The table has a bowl of brown sugar or a caster of granulated sugar. There is a pitcher of cream, a pot of sour cream, perhaps a bowl of unsweetened whipped cream, lemons and, for nuts like me, a peppermill. Now, everybody can dip and douse to their own satisfaction.

The shortcake will vary according to passionate regional preference, from cream biscuits, to scones, to what the cookbooks call shortcakes, to a sponge layer if you come from New York, as I do.

Iced tea embellished with the first sprigs of mint, or a puckering lemonade or beer is probably more traditional than wine; but it would not be too grave a break with tradition to serve a chilled—not icy—chardonnay. All are coolers for a bright and sunny day.

We will begin our feast late in the afternoon out of doors, on a screened porch or in a grange hall, eating until the late, around nine, onset of darkness when we set off fireworks or watch those of the town and thank our lucky stars for America.

KEEP THE HOME FIRES BURNING

I SOMETIMES THINK that if all the backyard barbecues in America were lit on the same hot and humid August night, smoke and a fine white ash would settle over the entire country. It's not all that improbable; we do seem to love a cookout.

When I was a child, eating out was mainly picnics with ants and blankets, but that may be because I was an apartment-dwelling city child without a garden to retreat to. The city isn't stopping anybody anymore who has a tiny terrace, a fire escape, a balcony or a roof. Once you leave the center of the city, every house must have a barbecue.

I think we love barbecues and grills because

they are informal. The fresh air sharpens our appetites, and there is something primitively appealing about an open fire and the smell of the smoke, the sizzling foods and the slightly charred taste.

There are problems with the barbecue parties. For the guests, soggy paper plates and insufficient napkins are the two worst. Hot and harried cooks, pinned to their fires, seem to suffer as much as they enjoy. Logistics for the go-befores and the go-along-withs can often seem haphazard. "Smoke gets in your eyes" isn't just a line from an old song.

Proper planning can solve the problems and restore the fun. Figure out where your prevailing wind comes from and place the barbecue so the smoke doesn't blow in the faces of cook or guests. If paper plates it must be, make sure they are large, coated so they don't leak, and as solid as possible so the food doesn't slip off as the guests wander.

I have found very inexpensive, colorful, spatterdashed enameled metal plates that can be used over and over without the risk of breakage. I really don't like plastic glasses; but if guests are walking around on a stone terrace or your barbecue is near a pool, I suppose they are essential. There are some permanent ones these days that are fairly solid with heavy bases so they are less liable to crack in people's hands and overturn. If there are tables and chairs, the glasses and silver can go on the table. Don't forget lots of large, colorful paper napkins. Barbecue foods tend to be messy.

In recent years, we have been encouraged to cook over practically anything that will burn, from mesquite (wood and charcoal), to vine cuttings to dried herbs such as fennel greens, as well as all manner of wood—dry or waterlogged—and exotica such as tea leaves. I suspect that most of us are still using charcoal or even gas grills.

It does pay to have some kindling and paper on hand. Getting the fire started and to the right stage by the time the guests are ready for you to cook is half the battle. I loathe and detest charcoal soaked in starter or starter sprinkled over the charcoal. The party and the food always smell of lighter fluid. Additionally, the liquid starters are dangerous. Keep a fire extinguisher around.

Make a little fire of paper and kindling. Once it starts, put on a few pieces of charcoal. When they catch, add the rest.

Our horizons have been expanded not only in fuel, but also in foods to put on the barbecue. Grilling no longer need mean that huge and costly steak or hamburgers and hot dogs with all their fat and cholesterol. We have been shown how to cook marinated pork roasts, small birds such as pigeons, chicken in pieces, whole fish (a wire cage to hold and turn the fish is a help), shrimp and vegetables.

Further changes can be rung by marinades and seasonings from oriental sesame oil, soy, ginger, garlic and rice wine vinegar to Greek oregano, thyme, lemon and olive oil. The world is your oyster. (By the way, oysters can go on the grill too, if well scrubbed. When they open, serve them with a little melted butter and pepper.)

Vegetables such as eggplant should be cut in half lengthwise and then scored so that the marinade or seasonings can sink in. Often, olive oil, salt and pepper are all that's needed. Zucchini, summer squash, peppers, mushrooms and slices of sweet potato and red onion all grill well, but do have a large spatula for turning them so they don't get squashed. Tongs will be fine for the meats.

I don't do all that. It's too hectic. I would never get to see my guests. One main course—perhaps one vegetable that can go toward the edge of the fire, and a hamburger or two for any children—is my absolute limit.

I like to have the rest of the food all cooked ahead and ready to set out. Nothing beats a platter of sliced tomatoes or tomatoes and onions with some pepper and a little olive oil. Nobody has come up with better treats than old-fashioned potato salad (although in today's world, you may want to use a low-calorie, low-cholesterol mayonnaise), and coleslaw, fragrant with celery seed. Both are better for a day of waiting in the refrigerator.

If you want to be more exotic, soak some tabbouleh, cracked bulgur wheat, in hot water; it needs no cooking. Then mix it with oil and lemon juice, chopped herbs and vegetables if you like.

Thinly sliced radishes, carrots and scallions—a little fennel would be nice—make a salad that doesn't wilt and can be given a zap of flavor with a lemon-based vinaigrette seasoned with ground cumin or chopped mint.

A spicy pot of beans can be made ahead and then kept warm in a low oven, or consider a black bean salad with orange juice, hot peppers and fresh coriander. Bread is an easy way to vary the look without work. Pita or papadums can be kept warm at the edge of the fire, or you can buy a loaf of interesting whole grain bread or individual corn muffins.

If you feel a first course is a must, try mugs of chilled soup. Dessert should follow the feel of the party, but don't serve cakes with rich icings that will melt and slip or ice cream and sorbet that will turn to soup. I usually make a big fruit salad or put out a bowl of berries and a plate of cookies and call it a day.

Have lots to drink. Chill it. Eating is thirsty work on a hot day. A large planter or even a wash bucket filled with crushed ice will do; but make sure that, even if you are having wine and beer, there is soda or pitchers of iced tea. Some people just don't like to drink and some are too young or are driving.

Oh, yes, finally figure out what you are going to do if it rains.

BAND-AIDS FOR THE
ONCE-A-YEAR COOK

MANY PEOPLE HAVE confessed to me in recent years that either they do not cook, cannot cook or no longer cook. I understand that cooking can seem intimidating if you've never done it or feel out of touch with past skills. What do you do with that great naked beast—the turkey—sitting on your counter? Some of us are proud of or feel required to make holiday meals. The holiday season may be the one time a year when we cook. Thanksgiving and Christmas are the most common such events. Certainly, even in my kitchen, it is when I make the most food at one time.

Even if we are harried, there are a few saving graces to the ritual. Good spirits are high and family and friends are prepared to enjoy themselves. They don't pick at the food or criticize the cook. We all tend to have a traditional repertoire that is repeated year after year and so the dishes are perfected; some of the tension disappears. Omitting traditional (your tradition) dishes is a risk.

There are things we can do to make our lives easier during this once-a-year rush. As more and better take-out stores and bakeries dot our landscape, we can fill in our menu with bought foods. Most of us buy bread unless we have a Southern family tradition of hot, quick breads. A variety of pies is purchasable. While I am vastly proud of my sour cherry pie, which I make with frozen cherries from the farmer's co-op—cherries that have been individually frozen without any sugar—I am less proud, perhaps because less fond, of my mince pie. I buy.

While I always make a cranberry dish— some years a mold, another a relish—I have one child who insists on cranberry sauce, the smooth kind, right out of the can. Who am I to tell her no? Other people may love to bake, but dislike soup-making. Canned soups can be doctored with liquor or herbs and spices, and good take-out soups are available in some places. Sometimes a favorite restaurant that doesn't normally do take-out can be persuaded to sell you a favorite dish.

In extremis, even cooked turkeys can be bought (sliced and reassembled) from various sources. Smoked turkey (ordered ahead) makes a reasonable alternative. However, turkeys are so easy to roast and relatively rapid as well if you follow my unconventional lead that there is really no excuse for not doing your own. The most important thing is to order an unfrozen, untreated turkey.

Remove any packet of innards, to use in a gravy or stuffing. In a microwave oven or on top of the stove, cook the neck—broken into a few pieces—and the gizzards with onion and, if you like, garlic, until the meat falls from the bone and you have a rich broth. Strain, and if you like a gravy with bits and pieces in it, pull the shreds of meat from the neck bones and chop the gizzards. The liver can now be sautéed, chopped and reserved for the gravy or it can be added to the stuffing.

Make your favorite stuffing. Incidentally, the recipes on bags of seasoned bread crumbs aren't bad. I, however, make a new one every year and have tried everything from couscous to bulgur wheat to cornbread and on as a base. Stuffings are very forgiving. Refrigerate the raw stuffing and either bake it later on its own, which makes serving easier and turns it into a dressing, or save it for stuffing the turkey.

Fifteen-pound turkeys are about an ideal cooking size. If you have a very large family, I would suggest two turkeys rather than one King Kong.

Bring the turkey to room temperature. Remove any gobs of fat. Either stuff or just salt and pepper the cavity and insert a couple of onions.

Put your oven rack at its lowest level and boost the bake setting temperature as high as it will go. You may have some smoke in the kitchen. But you will be rewarded by the juiciest, most quickly roasted turkey you have ever made, with the crispest skin.

I don't use a rack in the roasting pan; the bottom skin is hardly worth bothering about. I don't truss. Untrussed, the white meat and the legs will be properly done at the same time.

Counting backward from the time you want to serve the turkey, put it in the oven to allow for the cooking time plus one half hour.

Slide the turkey into the oven legs first. After fifteen minutes slide the turkey around with a wooden spatula so that it doesn't stick. Repeat moving the bird around about every twenty minutes. If the bird seems to you to be getting too dark before it is cooked, cover it with a tent of aluminum foil. Roast until the thigh joint near the backbone wiggles easily, which is about ten minutes before the turkey will be fully cooked.

An unstuffed nine-to-ten pound turkey will take about an hour and fifteen minutes, a twelve-pound one about five minutes more, a fifteen-pound one will go up to just under two hours, and a twenty-pound one takes three hours. If you are stuffing your turkey, add thirty minutes to which-ever cooking time applies.

Many of us are cooking for a good many fewer than the Norman Rockwell family, and even the small turkeys of today may be too big. In that case, use a half turkey breast, which will serve six. The best way to cook this small an amount is in the microwave oven, which provides no crisp skin, but is good for dieters.

Save the carcass and any bones on people's plates to make soup—my favorite part of the hol-idays. Cooking can be fun and maybe holiday success—made easy with these hints—will encour-age you to cook more than once a year.

CHRISTMAS PRESENT

IF SCROOGE WAS to have learned a lesson from his hideous night of Christmases past, present and future, it was that giving—not of expensive baubles, but of food and caring—permits us the right to share in the feast.

As a cook and writer about food, I may be more sensitized than most to the ceremonial and celebratory aspects of feasts, more conscious that they are meant to be a way of sharing and giving. In recent Christmas seasons as I and my harried friends bemoan the perils of shopping, the lack of time and the expense, I am driven to question—as so many do—the commercialization of all our holidays, the loss of a wider notion of giving.

Afraid of the world around us, many of us have withdrawn into a more and more circumscribed world in which presents are socially or, worse, professionally defined necessities. I suggest food as an antidote that is suitable and permits even those of us who have no religious affiliation to the holiday a response to the season. It gives us all a way of overcoming our sense of alienation and even impotence in the face of the horrors of our world.

We can move beyond the cans of food that our children are encouraged to bring to school. We can donate food, or better yet, cook at one of the numerous hospices, churches and centers that provide for the elderly, the poor, the ill and the outcast. Small children can help pack food for giving— yes, to friends, but more important to people we do not count on. We can include teenagers in the preparation and serving of food as a public benefaction.

We can think about friends or people whom we know less well who may be alone and invite them to join us. There used to be a time when no stranger in a church was allowed to leave without a feast to join. Today, we may be surrounded by strangers; but there is still an important meaning to the thought and act. We can ask friends or preachers for the names of people who might be better for an invitation.

One Christmas, as part of the New York

City Meals on Wheels project to feed the home-bound elderly, a group arranged to invite a large number of the elderly to a meal that was set up and hosted in a large supermarket. The most important part was arranging for the transportation and aid so that people who hadn't been out of their apartments—often one room—in years could attend. It was joyous.

Even in our own homes, the participatory preparation of food can establish traditions and a glow of accomplishment that will last far longer than the gimme-toys.

Pop corn and string it to festoon a tree. Make twice as much popcorn as the tree requires so everybody can munch as they go along. Raw cranberries make beautiful strings as well. Children too small to be trusted with a needle can be given strips of brightly colored construction paper to glue into a chain of rings.

By the time my children could stand, they participated in making gingerbread men. The kitchen and the children, aside from shorts and T-shirts, were stripped for action; people are easier to wash than clothes. For each cookie there was a lump of dough to pat out. When they were tiny, I helped with the cookie cutter and moved the shapes to cookie pans. Then from bowls, they helped themselves to raisins, nuts, dried cherries, ice cream sprinkles or M&M's. Sometimes a recogniz-able man or girl appeared; sometimes the designs were wild and woolly fantasies. Then into the oven and the wonderful smell of gingerbread filled the air. Sometimes we had figures missing an arm; but nobody seemed to care. We also made stars to tie with ribbon onto the tree.

As children got older, the figures got neater—not better—and we began to ask their friends to join the fun and I added a thin, white sugar icing to paint on after the cookies cooled. Now I find myself with large adults—those same children—cluttered around the same table, still wanting to join the fun.

The only problem with gingerbread is it doesn't last forever. So I also made the kind of water, flour and salt dough that is not meant to be eaten but can be baked hard and shellacked for permanent ornaments. At first, I rolled it beneath my palms into long ropes that the children could twist into ornate shapes as they pleased. Later they could make their own slightly grubby ropes.

On other days, we baked cookies and decorated tins. We made the traditional German cookies like pfeffernuesse that last for weeks. We made pomanders. I put a Band-Aid on the pushing finger as protection against the cloves as they were inserted into the oranges. We packed everything up to give as presents. Children realize that they don't have money of their own and this is a way that they can really give.

Sometimes something we do by accident

becomes a family tradition. I love braised leeks and made them to go with every turkey. One year I thought of making them; but I didn't seem to have time. Luckily, I had some leeks in the house because my son walked in, looked at all the food and immediately asked, "Where are the leeks?" I scurried to make them with the aid of my quick microwave. I realized I had started a tradition and now leeks were a permanent holiday tradition— not everybody's, but ours.

Making, giving, welcoming and sharing are all words that go well with food and with the holidays, harking back to a time when winter food was scarce and feasts were a promise of spring to come. Let's make sure that our Christmas "present" is one of real presents worth the giving.

TIRED

DESPITE THE POSSIBLE joys of holidays and the massive propaganda in song and advertising to convince us that holidays are times of universal love, warmth and happy entertainments with smiling children and jolly snowmen, I have heard too many family horror stories, listened to too many cases of the blues from the lonely and seen too many exhausted hosts and hostesses to be sure.

Even happy holidays and an excess of parties leave me tired and often a bit cranky. A sense of letdown and the need to get back to work both contribute. If I must also cook and—fortune forfend—even entertain, I am liable to feel put upon.

To make matters worse, I am usually suffering from the odd assortment of foods and drinks provided by a succession of creative party givers. I am tubby, tired and averse to food.

Usually, I love to have friends over, which is a lot nicer than trying to talk to them in noisy restaurants and worrying about the bill; but in the throes of after-the-party, I may just try to find a new restaurant and suggest we all go there. New restaurants can work as an excuse for a lack of homey hospitality.

If there is no escape, I set a simple table—this is no time for formal entertaining—and turn to my old staple recipes or cheat by gussying up prepared foods. After years of bitter experience, I have learned that attempts to jolly myself into a state of creativity when I am like this will only result in mucky-tasting foods with too many ingredients and resentment toward the guests. I've never had anybody complain about these from-the-scrum dinners, so I share them with you in case you are as weary and surfeited as I am.

I have two absolutely basic main courses, counted on through countless last-minute meals. Both of them are roasted and require cranking the oven up to its maximum temperature. One is a short leg of lamb, with the shoulder chops cut off and frozen for other meals. I stud the lamb with slivers of garlic and rub it with rosemary, salt and pepper. After the guests have arrived, I stick the lamb in the oven for about fifty minutes, which allows guests time for a drink and a first course before the lamb is ready.

Roast chicken works on the same principle, once I have removed the extra fat and stuffed the inside of each chicken with a halved lemon, several cloves of garlic and some fresh herbs, if I have them. I tend to allow one small chicken for each two people—two birds for four for instance—since I never seem to come out even between white- and dark-meat eaters.

Hoping that my guests are busy talking by the time I have to slip away, I remove either kind of meat to a platter. I skim the juices, put the roasting pan on top of the stove and deglaze it with a little wine—red or white, whatever's open—or broth.

The first course may be as simple as linguine with an olive-oil-and-garlic sauce or—horrors—tomato purée out of one of those paper containers, jazzed up with garlic and onion sweated in olive oil and dosed with dried herbs and pepper. A chunk of Parmesan and a grater on a plate are the finishing touch, not careful orchestrations of delicate decorations by professional gnomes. A little fresh basil couldn't hurt pasta either.

That's dinner, with lots of bread, a better red wine than the cooking deserves—a lubricant to amity—a salad, cheese and a yellow bowl of crisp-from-the-refrigerator apples or pears. When I'm in this mood, dessert lovers are out of luck unless I bought something.

A little more energy will provide a fruit sorbet. I keep jars of simple syrup on hand in the refrigerator. I purée whatever fruit is reasonably good, add a little lemon juice, and as much simple syrup as there is purée. I throw the whole thing in an automatic electric ice cream maker just before I bring in the roast.

A few new potatoes can be roasted in a covered pot with olive oil and garlic while the meat is cooking, if you think the meat will look too lonely.

If I'm driven to cocktails, I really cheat. A standby is Greek stuffed vine leaves from a can, drenched with fresh lemon juice and refrigerated. I plunk the contents into an attractive crock, add another filled with calamata olives, a third with cubes of feta and, if I have time, make some taramasalata in a blender with salmon roe, garlic, olive oil, lemon juice and a slice or so of white bread squooshed in warm water. Spoons, toothpicks and napkins are a necessity.

There are other good cheats. Purée a can of drained chick-peas with oriental (dark brown) sesame oil and a little garlic. Whirl skim-milk ricotta in a food processor with all the fresh herbs you can find—parsley and dill will be adequate—and some freshly ground pepper. Serve with either raw vegetables or crisped strips of pita.

Instead of dessert, create a strategic diversion by bringing out a decanter of Port and a bowl of walnuts with several nut-crackers. If you are an insane amasser as I am, add those useful tools of yesteryear, nutpicks, skinny metal skewers with pointed and bent tips that are perfect for getting out the elusive nutmeats that stick stubbornly in even the best-cracked of nuts.

I may even have convinced myself that having a few people over is possible: Where's the phone?

FROM LEMON TO
LETTUCE

A LEMON ADDICTION

I AM A citrus nut, a certified lemon fiend. When I set up in my kitchen to develop a new recipe or I go someplace to teach a class, by now my assistants know without being told that it is essential that they squeeze me a cup of lemon juice with which to work. It is as necessary to me as my ignominious, nongourmet, caffeine-laden diet soda. I have all sorts of valid rationalizations about the uses of acid in cooking: It helps to stabilize sauces; since it reinforces salty flavors, I can use less salt; it balances flavors both spicy and sweet; having fruit acid, it also compensates for the missing acid in less than perfectly ripe fruits and vegetables. As with all rationalizations, they are irrelevant. I am just happier when a dish has lemon juice in it. To me, citrus is a positive, upbeat seasoning.

I make my salad dressing with lemon juice and olive oil, a bit of kosher salt and a few grindings of black pepper. Fish and seafood are, to me, inedible without a squeeze of lemon or lime, which also does much for chicken, sautéed vegetables, veal stew and fresh strawberries as well as the more ordinary piece of melon. If I didn't already like beaches and semitropical climates, I think I would have to reconsider because of the prevalence of citrus in their foods.

Citrus grows plentifully in these climes, so it is a logical ingredient. It also serves as a mode of cooking without heat and as a balance to all the wonderful aromatic and hot seasonings. In more northern areas, we welcome citrus on sunny days. Lemonade, gin-and-tonic with a squeeze of lime and iced tea with lemon and orange juice and mint are practically the insignias of summer.

THE SEASONAL POTATO

BECAUSE POTATOES KEEP so well, we are used to thinking of them as a winter staple, thereby, except in summer-long potato salads, depriving ourselves of the special pleasure of thin-skinned, still slightly sweet—not all the sugar has become starch—freshly dug potatoes.

We are accustomed to thinking of round, red-skinned potatoes such as Red Bliss as new potatoes no matter how long ago they may have been dug. Technically, any potato—no matter what the color of its skin—that weighs less than three ounces and that is under three inches in diameter is a "new potato." I don't consider these new potatoes. I consider a true new potato to be one that has not grown to full size, has just been dug and hasn't developed a thick skin yet—much like a baby. These new potatoes will never have a mealy or floury flesh even if the variety is one that, when mature and aged, does have that kind of flesh and is perfect for baking and mashing.

In spring, I lay out my sprouted potato eyes—a good reason for buying organic potatoes that haven't been sprayed to prevent sprouting— under a blanket of hay instead of planting them under earth; that way, as the summer progresses, I can lift the straw and take out a few handfuls of the small, newly formed potatoes before laying the hay back down and letting the rest of them grow up. Some years, there aren't that many potatoes left for winter as I have ravaged the crop in infancy and adolescence. I have no regrets. I can always buy old potatoes.

When the potatoes are really small, the size of a large marble, they are called peewees or fingerlings depending whether they are round or elongated. I dump them into a fine mesh sieve and slosh them around vigorously under cold running water. The mesh and the water clean them without scrubbing. This is important as the skins are so tender they can be rubbed off with a coarse cloth. These are the potatoes I steam in butter.

I take a small saucepan just large enough to hold the potatoes with the lid firmly in place. I put in a knob of sweet butter and melt it over low to medium heat. I put in the potatoes and stir thoroughly. I put on the lid, and as the potatoes cook, from time to time I shake the pan, keeping the lid firmly in place with my other hand. After about seven minutes, I probe the potatoes with the point of a sharp knife. If it slides in easily, the potatoes are done.

Sometimes I salt and pepper them very lightly, sometimes I toss in some fresh chopped mild herbs such as dill, chives or chervil. The point is not to overwhelm the delicate taste of the potatoes. Always I serve them immediately so that they do not overcook and shrivel. If you have enough potatoes, this is splendid enough to be a dish on its own. Otherwise, fill out the plate with a simple piece of fish and some steamed green beans with sage.

I think these tiny potatoes are a luxury just as they are, and one of the few baby vegetables truly worth eating; but the lily gilders can stir in some sour cream, dill, fresh ground black pepper and good salmon (red) caviar. I won't insult you, or the caviar, by suggesting beluga.

As the potatoes get a little bigger in size, clean them by scrubbing with a rough cloth and proceed as above; but add a little water to the pan and cook somewhat longer—not sublime, but still superb.

These small potatoes are too good for potato salad. However, young potatoes that are firm and red-skinned with their organic skins left on will add extra pleasure to those salads that call for waxy potatoes such as German potato salad or the warm, French, pommes à l'huile. Larger, brown-skinned potatoes, like the ones grown commercially in Maine and on Long Island, are ideal for the mayonnaise-based, American potato salads. Even these will benefit from freshly dug potatoes, which will be firmer and less crumbly when cooked than their midwinter brethren.

Should you want to find some of the older, interesting potato varieties that are being farmed again, if in limited quantity, summertime is your best bet. Many of them are firm and waxy with smooth skins and have shapes more like a small cucumber than those we tend to think of for potatoes.

A variety of unusual potatoes, organically grown, are becoming available for planting and eating; but this trend only looks new. What we are actually doing is rediscovering the wide variety of potatoes that used to be available in America and around the world. The fabulous *Dictionnaire Vilmorin des Plantes Potagères* of 1947 lists almost fifty varieties of potatoes that can be dug from late May to October, and that includes types with white, yellow, violet and bicolored (even yellow and red) flesh. They even list the ratte, which has had a great vogue in Paris recently but was not in commercial production in 1947.

Incidentally, while yellow, white and red-fleshed potatoes typically keep their color when cooked, the violet or blue ones do not. However, if you cook the bluish-fleshed potatoes in the microwave, they will keep most of their startling color.

PEDIGREED OYSTERS

WE STARTED OUT with Bresse chickens, Smithfield ham, Kobe beef, Hawaiian pineapples and Madagascar peppercorns. Now virtually everything on "American" menus has a name, whether it be the place where the thing grows—Petaluma squab, Brae (the name of the farm) beef; the actual name of the grower—Mrs. Burbage's mint; the varietal name—Mrs. Burbage's mint; or the name of the gatherer or plucker—Mrs. Burbage's mint. Next, I expect to see designer foods.

Examples keep surfacing. In a restaurant, when I asked what the oysters were, I was told Flower oysters. My face must have reflected my incredulity. The waiter hastily explained: The oysters are farmed on the Long Island shore by a Mr. Flower who has named them after himself. In a French restaurant, deepwater oysters were named for the diver.

Indeed, a careful grower, often an organic one, is a quality assurance; and since Parma prosciutto has only recently been let back in the United States, I may be gratified upon finding out that I am eating an import rather than a domestic version.

The whole thing can get slightly ridiculous, especially since as a consumer, I may have little idea about the names and what they stand for. They could just as well be invented. Additionally, they imply quality in a slightly different way as if, indeed, it is my fault that I don't know what the names mean.

At the height of the oyster season and the holidays during which they are so frequently consumed, oysters are a perfect example of this, as they seem to come with as many names as wine, and the names refer to different things. Some refer to the place where the oysters are grown, some to the species—ten world-wide—only four are common in America. Some names are made up, which is no help at all.

Being from New York, I started young with oysters named after their port of origin, Blue Points (bloo pernts, as A. J. Liebling would have pointed out) from nearby Long Island. A period of living in Boston introduced me to Cape Cods. Little did I know then that these slowest-growing (five years to maturity) and best of East Coast oysters would be subdivided into naming by town: Wellfleet, Chatham and Wareham.

My first trip to Paris offered blissful instruction on the meaningful distinction between species rather than places: huître plate, a native European, true or flat-shelled oyster, and the huître creuse with its deep oval shells like most eastern seaboard, American oysters, but still a different variety. Until recently, they were often called Portugaises because the original spat, or seed, came from Portugal. In the 1970's, the Portugaises were nearly wiped out by disease and were largely replaced by a Pacific oyster, the Gigas, also grown on the Northwest coast of the U.S. These oysters are not as good as the old Portugaises.

The French also identify oysters by place names. Many of the true oysters were called Belons after a particularly prestigious bit of Brittany, although recently the use of this name has been extended to any flat Breton oyster.

Other huîtres creuses were called fines-de-claire, having been raised in special flat ocean basins such as that at Marennes. However, if an oyster is actually called a Marennes, it probably has a hint of iodine in the flavor and slightly green hue.

Moreover, I had to learn that these Europeans came in sizes 000 to 4 for the flat oysters and 1 to 4 for the Portugaises. The lower the number, the bigger and more expensive. I was very proud of my knowledge, which was certified and rewarded with a midnight pig-out on New Year's Eve.

Years later, a particularly nasty London winter with the last of the pea-soup fogs—I couldn't find my car for three days—was ameliorated by my discovery of British oysters. I ate them when I could afford them, which was sadly seldom. These oysters were round and flat like my French loves and were named after the towns from which they came. My favorites were the Colchesters. I didn't yet know that there was a greater snobbery in appreciating the Colchesters called Pyefleets, from the Pyefleet creek. There are native British oysters, such as the Royal Whitstables, and then those grown from Brittany seed oysters.

Naming oysters by where they are grown makes much sense. Unfortunately, it can also conceal important changes. Today, a high percentage of the huîtres creuses in France are no longer Portugaises, but instead a related species from the Pacific—not as good.

Jim Beard introduced me to the tiny Olympias, the only indigenous American true oyster, no bigger than a thumbnail. They came from his native Oregon; but I had much to learn about other West Coast oysters, deep, oval and frilly, grown from Pacific (originally Japanese) seed as well as some from European seed, up and down the West Coast from Hog Island on Tomales Bay in California up through Yaquina Bay in Oregon; in Washington, in Wescott Bay on San Juan Island, in Shoalwater and Willapa bays, and Quilcene and Hama Hama in the Hood Canal, all the way up to Lasqueti Island in British Columbia. Then there is another Japanese oyster, known as kumamoto, with a small, almost conical shell also harvested in the Northwest.

From the eastern shore come Absecon (a spot near Atlantic City) oysters big enough to eat with a knife and fork, the Apalachicolas (Florida's Gulf coast), the Chincoteagues (Virginia), Cotuits (Massachusetts) and Malpeques (Prince Edward Island).

European flat oysters are grown on both coasts, often under the misleading place-name of Belon. Worse complications may yet be in the wings as we begin to get a separate species of true oysters in from Chile.

Just this summer, I had to confront Ireland's wide diversity of excellent oysters, flat and oval species from Kinsale to Galway.

While some gourmets more discerning than I may be able to keep in mind the identity of a taste to go with each of the oyster species and locations, and while it's nice when well-trained waiters know which oyster is which—pointing to the oyster assortment—I don't like being inundated by unsolicited and condescending information. (The other day, at a well-known restaurant, a noted food editor and I were informed how to eat our food.)

What we need to develop is a new menu nomenclature for oysters that gives at least as much information as a good wine list. Oysters are like California wine, not Bordeaux. We have to be told the oyster species. Then we should be given the region, with its state or country included, and, perhaps, even a word or two characterizing the color, size and flavor.

In the meantime, I will continue to enjoy all sorts of oysters in cold months, asking only that they come from clean water. Oysters are one of the few foods for which I am willing to risk my health.

SCIENCE AND THE
SUMMER'S SAUCE

TODAY'S COOKS AND eaters are deeply
split in their attitudes toward science. There was a
time around the turn of the century when many
cookery writers and teachers brought what they
considered to be science into the kitchen in an attempt to lighten women's workload and to give it
more status. In those days, science was the god.
Even then, there were intimations that not all
viewed the possibilities of science sanguinely. Both
Dr. Jekyll and Mr. Hyde and *Frankenstein* portrayed
evil abuses of science; but when Dr. Harvey
Kellogg of Battle Creek told us that cornflakes
were a health food, we believed.

In recent years, our belief in science when

joined to food has plummeted. We have come to fear the influence scientists have on our food, bringing our attitude close to the level of paranoia. At a meeting of serious food people, one has only to say "processed" to evoke a frenzy of negative feelings. With some reason, we look on all sprays and chemical additions to the soil with suspicion. We are not happy when scientists juggle genes to change the taste, productivity and durability of food; but where would we be if previous generations of experimenters had not created large red tomatoes, cultivated strawberries and strong, disease-resistant corn?

I'm sure that none of us wants to go back to the pre-Pasteur days of contaminated milk; but we wince at the idea of shelf-stable, irradiated foods whether our European friends have been using them for years or not. I for one am unwilling to give up my refrigerator.

Most of us use our freezers, but apologetically. While blind tastings and common sense have shown that, in many cases, frozen fish is better than what is deemed to be fresh, we still take the phrase "fresh fish" as an assurance of quality. We may know that fishing boats go out to sea for weeks at a time and that their heavily iced cargoes are no fresher than fish frozen immediately upon being caught; but some part of our souls refuses to believe it.

We welcome the very modest price due to

scientific breeding, raising and feeding of today's chickens, which have become a staple rather than the luxury they were in the past; but we are rightly horrified by outbreaks of salmonella, even if it is not clear that yesterday's chickens were safer. Chicken needs to be cooked. The free-ranging chickens of the past were indeed leaner and had more flavor than the battery-farmed ones of today. (By the way, what has happened to all the stewing fowl and tough cocks that once were used for long-cooked savory dishes?)

While this same intensive, "scientific" breeding may be responsible for recent problems with eggs used raw, science can also help.

Fortunately, an intelligent, scientifically trained writer on reactions culinary—think alchemy—has come to the rescue. Harold McGee has figured out that, with short bursts of cooking, it is possible to heat acidulated egg yolks—with water and lemon juice—to a salmonella-killing temperature without coagulating them. Therefore, following his model, it is once again possible to make safe mayonnaise.

The mayonnaise will have a slight flavor of cooked egg yolk as in a Hollandaise or a custard; but it is still infinitely preferable to commercial substitutes unless you are making American potato salad or coleslaw.

The procedure is a bit of a pain and requires a microwave oven. If you want to know more about it, have a low-wattage oven or live in the mountains, read *The Curious Cook*. In the meantime, with Harold's kind consent, I have turned his formula into kitchen instructions.

Separate two large eggs, saving the whites for another purpose. Put the yolks in a two-cup glass measure and whisk thoroughly with two tablespoons plus one teaspoon each of water and lemon juice. Wash the whisk with very hot, soapy water. Cover the measure tightly with microwavable plastic wrap. Cook at 100 percent power for thirty seconds in a 650- to 700-watt oven (800 watts if using new ovens with the new standards applied). Prick plastic. Remove from oven. Uncover. Whisk with cleaned whisk. Return to oven uncovered and cook for twenty seconds. Remove from oven. Whisk with a *clean* whisk—yes, again—until cool. Now continue whisking in oil as if making any other mayonnaise. Use one and one-half cups of the oil of your choice, seasoning to taste with salt and pepper, and mustard if desired: scientifically safe mayonnaise.

A LITTLE BIT OF PIG

PORK AND ITS descendants—ham, ham
hocks, salt pork, lard, bacon, bacon grease, sausages, fresh ham and pork chops—which used to
be the great meat staples of the American diet have
been disappearing from our tables and our recipes
except in the American South, and with the excep-
tion of spare ribs and a few other Chinese dishes. It
is understandable that as settler societies got richer
in the mid-nineteenth century, they turned from
what was seen as a humble meat to upscale beef,
newly, reasonably available from the great ranch-
lands.

We have continued to turn away from pork,
fearing its fat and, in cured meat, its nitrates and

nitrites. We have become scared of a mostly myth-ical trichinosis (there have been few new reported cases). We have also created new problems as eager pork raisers have tried to comply with our osten-sible desire for leaner meats by raising leaner pigs, and as indices for increased internal temperatures of cooked pork have been given in the quest for greater safety. Consequently, our pork is drier, less succulent, less attractive and, if not cooked very carefully, tough. Earlier recipes, which were based on fatter pork, will give poor results.

Today, we must look for recipes that call for only brief sautéing, broiling, roasting or grill-ing, and then proceed to finish cooking at lower heat, with a fair amount of liquid, which can be provided by vegetables, to keep the pork moist. Old-fashioned smothered, stewed and braised pork dishes could be revived if low heat is used through-out a shortened cooking time. Official guidelines say that pork should be cooked to at least 160°F, even though trichina die around 140°F. It is also believed that eaters will not tolerate pork that is at all rosy inside.

I myself cook a boned and rolled loin of pork placing the bones in the pan on either side of the roast in a 500°F oven for fifty minutes. This works no matter how much the roast weighs as the roast only gets longer; it doesn't get thicker. If you can't bear pink meat, cook the roast for fifteen minutes longer. The pan can be deglazed with anything from orange juice to red wine to make a light gravy. The roast can be seasoned by being stuck with cloves of garlic, chopped herbs, needles of rosemary and/or pieces of fresh sage leaves. Suddenly, we remember how good pork is and cheap.

Nevertheless, we are losing a lot of delectable recipes: stuffed pork shoulder, crown roast of pork, fresh ham and stuffed pork chops just for starters. We are also losing pork as an enrichment, that little bit of pig that got me started thinking along these lines altogether.

James Beard firmly maintained that chicken dishes, especially stocks and soups, needed a little pork to be at their best. I don't know if he had this idea because he grew up in a house with a Chinese chef, Jue Let. As I understand it, Chinese cooks who want to go the extra mile and make "superior stock" always add pork bones and a bit of ham to their pots. The Yunnan ham they add tastes much like our Smithfield hams.

Using a little pork with an alien meat such as chicken or beef is not as exotic as it may seem. The French, in their rich, long-simmered stews, used to put a large square of rind from good smoky bacon at the bottom of the pan. This served three purposes. It kept the stew from sticking and burning. It added gelatin from the skin and a nice smoky background taste that was often reinforced by browning the meat at the beginning of the cooking in some bacon fat that had been rendered from lardoons (sautéed sticks of bacon). The lardoons were added back into the stew at the end as a flavor-filled crunch.

Any of us who cook Chinese food will quickly come to the conclusion that a little bit of pig is a necessity. It seems that every dish that is neither vegetarian nor dessert has pork of some kind in it, from lobster Cantonese to winter melon soup.

In Bordeaux, raw oysters are served with hot slices of spicy sausage. The Spanish add sausage to paella made with seafood and chicken. The Portuguese add it to vegetable and bean soups.

In French cooking, the kind of lardoons made for stews, the warm fat from rendering them and a good red wine vinegar are used to make the frisée (young, whitish green chicory) salad that is one of the joys of bistro cooking.

In America, we used to make wilted salads, particularly of spinach, with warm bacon fat, which was also a normal fat for sautéing potatoes and all sorts of wonderful, unhealthful foods. During World War II, it was considered patriotic, not parsimonious, to have cans with pork drippings ready for cooking. Extras got donated to the war effort.

Many other somewhat bitter greens, in addition to those in salads, benefit from the soothing richness of pork fat. Italians cook broccoli rabe—more greens than florets—with the fat from sausages as well as olive oil. Sauté three-quarters of a pound of broccoli and four tablespoons of fat from sautéing Italian pork sausages or olive oil along with five cloves of garlic for about seven minutes. Then add one-half cup of liquid—water or broth— and simmer covered for a half hour. Serve with the sausages cooked to yield fat or with grilled sausages if you started with olive oil.

Southern greens—collards, turnip greens, beet greens, mustard greens, kale, pokeweed— cook for an even longer time, up to four hours, with a split ham hock or two. The cooked greens and the meat from the bones are then served up with corn bread and pleasure. The potlikker (cooking liquid) can be served as a soup or a spring tonic. The French version calls for spring-tender dandelion greens, cooked possibly with sliced green onions in the bacon-fat-and-lardoon model. The difference from the frisée salad is that the greens are cooked and there's no vinegar. The Chinese cook dark greens to serve with hard sausages or make them into a soup with slivers of ham.

Spring is a particularly good time to consider the marriage of pork and strong-tasting greens, since historically they were either foraged wild at this time of year or they were available from the garden where they had wintered over.

We will probably never see the widespread return of lard crusts, once considered the flakiest and most tender, nor will suet pudding figure on many festive tables. Breakfast will have to go on without eggs and butter-soaked grits being based on a thick, fried ham steak with red-eye gravy made by deglazing the iron cooking skillet with strong coffee.

However, even if we must limit our intake of pork—particularly cured pork—beans can continue to be baked with a lump of bacon or salt pork or boiled with a ham bone and vegetables. A little pig splendidly carries and rounds out all kinds of flavors from sweet to spicy.

RECIPE BABIES IN
CABBAGE PATCHES

SOMEHOW, NO MATTER how much I want to talk about reality, I end up speculating about trends. It is hard to think of cabbage as trendy—Mrs. Wiggs, Peter Rabbit, French babies, cole slaw and bubble-and-squeak are my associations—but the comfort in these images is exactly what is wooing people back to cabbage. Many of us are tired of chasing after the newest hottest exotica. Cabbage has been so out that it is turning into a novelty. It is clearly destined for superstardom, on the cusp of trend and nostalgia.

There were reasons people avoided cabbage: its lingering odor when overcooked, its reputation as a poverty food—the one cheap green vegetable available all winter long, often preserved as a vat of homely sauerkraut. Why certain culinary cultures boiled fresh cabbage to death is hard to understand; but quickly sautéed, lightly simmered or braised, the vegetable is gentle, elegant, richly rewarding. Most cuisines—from Irish to Russian to Japanese—have classic cabbage recipes that can serve as inspiration. Preserved cabbage, sauerkraut and kimchee were major winter sources of vitamin C along with potatoes.

In stores, we have a wider spectrum of cabbages to choose from than we ever had before. There are big, round, green Savoys, crinkled and decorative, with tender leaves and a mild taste. There are standard cabbages—either young, mild and pale green, or large midwinter cabbages whose outer leaves vary from dark green to almost purple. We have red cabbages, really a deep purple, which always need some acid—wine vinegar or citrus—when cooked to maintain their brilliant beetlike color (and not turn a nasty gray). There is paler, cylindrical Napa cabbage, which used to be called bok choy. Today bok choy is the name speakers of Cantonese use for Mandarin Chinese cabbage, whose pale ribs are frilled with dark green leaves. Savoys, Napas and standard cabbages are fairly interchangeable—except for the red, which stains everything around it and has a darker, winier taste. Napa and Savoy cabbages need a briefer cooking time than the standard.

I myself cook cabbage in two opposing fashions: One is a quick vegetable dish, a light sauté or stir-fry to go with grilled foods or underneath steamed fish—it usually surprises guests, and pleases them. (A passing thought: Never use an aluminum pan when cooking cabbage—the pan will give the cabbage an unpleasant taste.)

On the other hand, there are days when I want to serve an all-out extravaganza that lets all my guests know: "I have dined today." My idea of an extravaganza is one of the great traditional composed dishes, steaming, aromatic, succulent and delivering a range of textures, such as a chartreuse of pheasant and cabbage adapted from a classic recipe. Traditionally, it was a molded, layered dish of vegetables and meats making a decorative pattern. Sometimes a chartreuse is held together with forcemeat (the finely chopped, highly seasoned meat used for stuffings).

Lest you still think that cabbage must be only homely or fatty, consider red cabbage with salmon. It looks beautiful and its flavors are intense.

REALLY RADICCHIO

IT USED TO be that when a cheap restaurant wanted to bulk up and class up a truly abysmal salad it would slice in some red cabbage. A similar thing has happened to high-priced greens as they are joined on the plate by the expensive, similarly purple-red leaves of radicchio. I ask myself if they are there for taste, snobbery or simply a change of color. As I read new American recipes calling for a leaf of radicchio in the presentation, I am haunted by the "lettuce cups" of yesteryear. It is too bad that a really sensational vegetable is being abused merely for its color. In any case, the question may not be, "Why radicchio?" but, "Which radicchio?"

Radicchio is the Italian name for a good-sized group of red chicories, not lettuce. I once wasted a good deal of time at the London branch of Sutton Seeds hunting in the lettuce section only to be finally admonished, in reply to a query, that what I was looking for was chicories, but that Sutton's, a true-blue English house, did not carry them. The blow was slightly softened by a suggestion that I try red butterhead lettuce. I did; but, excellent as the elegant, soft leaves were, they could not replace the fleshy, slightly bitter chewiness of the radicchios.

I soon discovered that there was not one but a plethora of radicchios. All are named after the towns in the Veneto where they are primarily grown. The one we have seen so much of in recent years, the dark red ball that looks like an undernourished cabbage, is Rosso di Verona (Rouge de Vérone). The many other kinds have been unavailable, but are beginning to come into the stores. Additionally, some of the less common radicchios are being commercially grown in America, and seed is available from various sources.

The radicchio that the Italians eat most is Treviso. It is the color of the Verona variety, but its leaves are longish, sort of gawky, adolescent Belgian endive leaves. When you realize that the head looks like a disorderly head of endive, it doesn't take long to figure out that this kind of chicory is related to endive; but whereas the blanched, second-growth (growing on the winter-hardy roots left after the first growth of leaves has been cut back) endives turn white in the dark, the similarly treated radicchio turns yet a darker red, its white veins standing out in gaudy splendor. The first time I planted Treviso I knew nothing about its special requirements. I planted it in the spring along with my other seeds. All I got for my troubles were long, thin, dark green, very bitter leaves. Verona radicchio is grown in the same way as Belgian endive. In both cases, the blanching produces not only the color, but also a waxy leaf with a milder flavor.

Field-grown radicchios—not forced second growth—are Variegata di Chioggia (the *ch* has a hard sound) and Variegata di Castelfranco. Both of these are mottled (variegated) red and white like American cranberry beans. Chioggia has a more pronounced color and white ribs; it forms semioval heads that are somewhat loosely packed, while Castelfranco really looks like a soft, roundish leaf lettuce. To further confuse the issue, Chioggia is sometimes forced, in which case the heads become waxier and look like indecisive Treviso. There are many other varieties, such as Palla Rossa and Sottomarina, and even one called Chiavari, grown mainly for its edible root; but I have never eaten, grown or cooked this last kind so it remains, to me, the leaves of myth.

All of the radicchios are late-season, winter

lettuces. They do not take freezing weather; but they do need temperatures in the low forties to really develop a brilliant color. If they get early snow cover, many will survive quite cold temperatures. When I have gone to ski resorts in Italy and nearby, hard-to-differentiate Austria (Alto Adige or Sud Tirol—it depends when Austria had possession) late in the ski season, I have frequently had the first tiny, not yet unfurled leaves of radicchio whose seed was planted very late in the fall to come up in the low-lying towns at the mountains' base with the first departure of snow.

Radicchio can be used as a mesclun, a collection of early unheaded lettuce. If you start the seeds in a warm window in winter and then move them to a window in an unused room, the radicchios may turn red for you. Pick the leaves as soon as they are about two inches tall. Aside from this use of early leaves, Italians almost never use any of the radicchios in a mixed salad, but savor them alone with the simplest of olive oil dressings.

The mature leaves tend to be chewy and don't go well with tender lettuce. There is one splendid mixed salad made with Verona and thinly sliced bulb (Florence) fennel.

More often, Italians cook radicchios, usually turning to the non-Verona varieties, which are milder in flavor as the bitterness of radicchio intensifies with cooking. It is a tonic bitterness that is extremely agreeable as a contrast to rich or fatty flavors. These radicchios are braised, grilled, stirred into risottos and stewed. If we abandon radicchio as a splash of red in salad and try traditional recipes, we may lose a salad but gain a terrific vegetable.

THE TIP OF THE
ICEBERG

BRAVELY, I ADMIT I like iceberg (Simpson) lettuce; I buy it; I eat it. I eat it the way I did as a child, cut into crisp wedges and slathered with delicious tacky Russian dressing made with about two parts commercial mayonnaise to one part commercial chili sauce. I eat this salad with a knife and fork. I wouldn't think of putting another kind of lettuce on my tuna sandwich.

Even worse from the food snobs' point of view, I often enjoy a salad, made in winter, with torn chunks of iceberg lettuce, lots of thinly sliced white onions and a dressing of olive oil, lemon juice, salt and pepper. This salad is even better after it is allowed to get a little soggy for twenty minutes or so. If you want to add some Boston lettuce, feel free.

By this point, I have probably lost all my credentials as a gourmet or even a good cook. In my defense, I note that while iceberg lettuce has lost all cachet as a salad green, even the snobbiest still seem willing to use it to wrap Chinese minced squab, Thai specialities or, shredded, as a garnish for Southwestern food.

Aside from the carefully shielded red radicchios, blanched endive and expensively transported lettuce from distant soils, most of us can only look forward by late fall to deficiencies in the salad greens department. Lettuce that has been packed in ice for shipping has strange tastes and textures. Plastic-encased baby lettuce leaves are very expensive although a work saver as they don't need washing.

Maybe this salad situation will get some people to look at iceberg lettuce again. It is available all winter as it keeps very well. It is almost never dirty. All that has to be done to it is to insert a sharp knife at the stem end and make a deep conical incision so that the core can be removed—as if a cabbage were being cleaned. Then remove any browned, limp or faded external leaves. The lettuce should be torn apart or have its leaves separated, depending on the way it is to be used. The only time it is cut with a knife is for those old-fashioned hearts-of-lettuce wedges. They must be eaten immediately. Cutting the lettuce makes it discolor quickly.

Of course, one can go too far with iceberg lettuce. It should not be ubiquitous. In a very trendy, resuscitated restaurant in London, I was served a Caesar salad with iceberg lettuce. No, no, no . . . I am a purist here at least. It must be romaine or, as the Brits would call it, cos. Midwinter, romaine gets very large and darkly green. This does not make an ideal Caesar salad either. Self-restraint must be exercised. Use only the inner, pale and crisp leaves. The dark leaves that are left over make a terrific soup if finely shredded, wilted in a little butter with some thinly sliced onion and then simmered with good chicken broth. It can be puréed if desired and salt and pepper added as wanted. Cream-soup freaks can stir in some cream whisked with an egg yolk and then simmer until thickened.

While a Caesar will never be a health food salad, it can be made relatively safe by using vinegar instead of lemon juice, using only one egg and thinning the egg mixture, after cooking, with a little water.

Speaking of fat-loaded dressings, I have another far-from-fashionable favorite that does wonderfully on iceberg lettuce wedges. Again, it's based on mayonnaise from the jar. Just whisk in some good, creamy blue cheese, leaving some chunks, but no large cubes. Use a Midwestern blue like Navoo, or some Gorgonzola. Don't use Roquefort—it's too salty—or Stilton—a waste.

Having burned my respectability bridges, I will now defend American mayonnaise. It isn't olive-oil rich and eggy like homemade and respectable mayonnaise; but, on that tuna sandwich—yes, canned tuna—I want my childhood mayo.

The same holds true for deviled eggs, egg salad, many kinds of chicken salad, a BLT, a club sandwich and my summer favorite, the eaten-over-the-sink sliced tomato and mayo sandwich on soft white commercial bread. It's more than nostalgia, it still tastes wonderful.

If I could peek in the refrigerators of my purist friends, I wonder how many would reveal the familiar fat jar. Before I learned about canning, I used to boil the jars and lids and save them for summer preserves. Now, I save them only for refrigerator storage; but I never throw them out.

Even if I convince no one to go for iceberg lettuce and mayo, I may give heart to those, like me, still sneaking these delights in private. Would I serve the hearts-of-lettuce-with-Russian at a dinner party? No, I'm not retro enough for that. I probably wouldn't serve it to my family either because of the fat; but they have often eaten the iceberg lettuce salad in winter. Bravely, if there is no labor problem reason not to, let's make Eat Iceberg buttons and wear them in public.

PERFECT POSH: THE FABULOUS FOODS

THERE ARE FOODS whose very names conjure up luxury as do the artifacts of their fantasy world: candles glittering in heavy silver candelabras, crystal glasses so thin that it seems an unkind word would shatter them or so heavy that their hand-cutting magnifies the candlelight by hundreds, white damask napkins large enough to be cloths for a small table, and rare china embellished piece by piece with vivid designs and leaf of purest gold. In this dream world, the women rustle with long gowns of taffeta and glisten with costly stones. The men wear black tie with matching ribboned pumps. Their jackets do not have shawl collars.

Fortunately, in the real world, these foods carry their luxury with them without benefit of gilding. They are the making of the most sumptuous breakfast in bed, a dinner for a cherished other sprawled in front of a fireplace and brunch with a few good friends and all informality. One reason they are so adaptable is that they need no cooking. Of course, they make perfect presents. Then you can leave the setting up to someone else.

What are these foods? Much pleasant thought suggests: caviar and smoked sturgeon, smoked salmon, foie gras, and white and black truffles, pâtés and Stilton, whole glazed chestnuts and dates worth swapping your camel for.

No food's name or presence breathes the extravagant life in quite the same way as caviar. In our dreams, this caviar has large plump eggs, each discrete with no oil floating, no crushed eggs. The eggs are gray-black or black-brown, and come via Russia or Iran from very large, beluga sturgeon and are processed with a minimum of salt, malassol. If indeed your life is about to be blessed with such an indulgence, you will need little beyond small plates and spoons that are not metal or that are gold plated, since other metals contaminate the taste of caviar. In the old days, kilo containers of caviar used to be shipped with mother-of-pearl spoons crossed on top. Today, you will have to buy your own. They can be vermeil, mother-of-pearl, shell or horn. There are other trappings of caviar elegance; double bowls to keep the caviar nestled in ice and ice buckets that do the same for Champagne or vodka.

A tall glass of Champagne—yes, I would buy the very best French; no point in stinting now—or small icy glasses or, even better, Russian silver cups to sip from is the only essential accompaniment of first-class caviar. For me, the Champagne glass should be slim, elegant and thin with long stems so my hand doesn't warm the small, tight, cold bubbles.

You don't need lemons, chopped eggs and—fortune forbid—chopped onion. If your caviar is not perfect, serve strips of white toast without crusts and some lemon. Traditionally, it is only jammy, thick, pressed caviar or salmon caviar that get blini, those puffy, yeast-raised, slightly sour, white or buckwheat flour Russian pancakes. Even the very good caviar from other smaller sturgeon— the Caspian sevruga and osetra, the American heckleback—deserve to be tasted seriously. If there is more caviar than I can eat plain or need to stretch what I have, the only thing I like is a crusty baked potato, split and smashed to make it mealy and lavished with sweet butter and sour cream. Divide the caviar between the white creamy mounds and give guests knife and fork.

The only caviars to cook with are golden American whitefish caviar and salmon caviar. They both have firm membranes protecting their liquid insides and so won't mush with moderate heat. It is a shame to waste really good caviar in cooking; it also doesn't cook well. Lumpfish caviar, which is sometimes recommended, should be avoided. It is dyed and will turn anything you mix a ghastly green-black color.

Caviar is the most apparent luxury. However, even after you have decided to loosen your purse strings, many decisions remain. You must decide what fish you are going to deprive of progeny. Most people mean sturgeon eggs when they say "caviar"; but caviar can honorably come from a salmon, a trout or, heaven help us, a snail. Even if you know that you want those wonderful, expensive black eggs that come from sturgeon, there are still questions to ask yourself before the big purchase.

First, do you want to be personally responsible for increasing the national debt and adversely affecting the trade balance? Historically, the best caviars have come from the Caspian Sea, either caught and processed by Russians or Iranians. Today, there is caviar from mainland China. These add political questions to the ones of economics and quality. The reason you have to decide is that while America has very good caviar of many kinds and hues, its sturgeon eggs come from cousins of the Caspian's dwellers. It's like comparing sheep's milk cheese with goat's milk cheese, both good but different. The best American caviar, almost comparable in quality to beluga, comes from Pacific white sturgeon and is extremely limited in quantity. Heckleback is also a true sturgeon; but paddlefish is a distant relative and the caviar isn't as good.

It's nice to know that the golden caviar can be frozen. The others should be kept to the rear of the lowest shelf in the refrigerator where it is coldest and eaten within a week of purchase. You cannot keep caviar as cold as a good purveyor does without freezing it. Once you open your precious tin or jar, the best thing is to greedily gobble up your supply. If there are leftovers, cover them tightly with plastic wrap before putting the top back on the container.

The prices may alarm you; but they shouldn't be confusing. The quality-price ratio is practically absolute. If you see beluga, the most expensive and largest-egged caviar, that is surprisingly inexpensive, it is probably vacuum packed, not fresh. This is like the difference between a sweet-smelling fresh raspberry and a frozen one. Sometimes, right after the holidays, stores that do a large business in caviar will have too much inventory and sell it at a discount, and I might spoil myself. Give me a jar of caviar, my love, and cold Champagne and I will stay in bed all through the day.

*   *   *

The fish, sturgeon, from which all those delicious eggs come is a delicacy in its own right. In Russia, it is prized as a cooking fish. The firm flesh is usually prepared in a soup called solianka, creating a rich golden broth. When settlers first came to America, the rivers were dense with sturgeon. They were caught in vast quantities and were not thought of as anything special. Now that they are scarce, most of us still don't cook sturgeon; but when it is gently smoked, turning the flesh white and the thin layers of fat golden, the fish becomes an expensive fragile treat. It is best served on its own without even toast or lemon. You might grind a tiny amount of fresh pepper on top. If there are no limits set on my gluttony, I top thin slices of smoked sturgeon with spoonfuls of caviar; the sturgeon should be at room temperature, the caviar cold. The drinks are still Champagne or vodka, although you might consider a flinty Chablis. I prefer vodkas with a taste, potato vodkas. My favorite is Kord from Czechoslovakia; also Luksusowa from Poland and Rimanto from Germany, all good.

Unlike caviar, almost all of the sturgeon we eat is American. The very best we have had is the Pacific white. Until recently, sturgeon has been defined as a game fish in California and therefore unfishable in that state. All the flesh and caviar from this wonderful sturgeon has come from farther north—the Columbia River. Newly available farm fish will be easier to deal with.

When you buy smoked sturgeon in a store, the flesh should look moist and not stringy. It should be cut in broad, unbroken diagonal slices and the fat layers should be golden and firm. A tasted piece should melt in your mouth. Since the flesh is pale, when serving use a plate with a colored but delicate pattern. This is food too elegant for my usually favored, peasanty plates. If you have them, fish knives and forks would be perfect.

Smoked salmon may be America's favorite smoked fish. It should be very lightly smoked. Its slices should be thin to the point of translucency and large from careful diagonal cutting. The beautiful color will vary in intensity from the palest Norwegian salmon to the strong color of the different breed of Northwestern salmon.

The most expensive smoked salmon has always been line-caught, Scotch river salmon. These fish have had to work, fighting their way upstream to spawn, and are less fatty than the sea-farmed Norwegian kind. The Scotch fish are very light on salt. When in prime condition, this assures the most elegantly extraordinary delicacy. Unfortunately, such delicacy suffers if stored too long. Always buy Scotch salmon from a source that sells lots of it and cares about its reputation. If you buy or have been gifted with a whole side, you will find that it is considerably smaller than other sides of smoked salmon. It will weigh between three and a half and six pounds. Unless the salmon has been presliced, you will have to arm yourself to the task. The procedure is the same no matter what kind of salmon you have.

First, you will need a long, thin, flexible knife known, oddly enough, as a smoked-salmon knife. You will need a good pair of tweezers or a small, needle-nosed pliers. Place the cold salmon skin side down on a board. With your knife held parallel to the surface of the fish, remove any hard edges and the yellowish, shiny surface layer. (Waste not, enjoy more; save your parings to boil with new potatoes and serve as a first course with a little melted butter, sour cream and finely chopped dill or chives.) Marching down the fish, parallel to the backbone, are two lines of small "pin" bones. If you run your fingers up and down the fish, you will feel the bone tips poking out. Each line will have many small bones that should be pulled out with the tweezers or pliers. Next, lay the fish—still skin side down—with the tail toward your nonknife hand. With the knife in your other hand, the blade held fairly flat to the board, cut slices that are as thin and broad as possible toward the head end. It's much like cutting a flank steak.

The traditional accompaniments for smoked salmon are buttered slices of thin brown bread, wedges of lemon, pepper from a mill and even capers. Once again, the better the fish, the less you should put with it. There are two other simple possibilities: Whip some heavy cream and fold in white prepared horseradish to taste, or have an attractive cruet of a very good, but not overly green and heavy olive oil available. If the fish is a little dry, a slick of the oil will moisten it.

Norwegian farmed salmon is considerably lighter in color and fattier than Scotch. The Northwestern is darker in color and stronger in taste. The Norwegian is best on canapés and sandwiches. The Northwestern is good on its own and with eggs. The most elegant served as a first course on translucent china and with a thin flute of Champagne, is Scotch or Irish.

It is very hard to tell you why truffles, those underground growers, are so famous, so sought after, so expensive. Knowledge of their hiding places is a fiercely protected family secret. There are dark midnight rumors about the rituals surrounding the search. It is certainly their addictive smell that is the first element in their success. Animals trained to hunt them are led on by the special perfume; but they do demand a taste of the truffles as a reward. The tastes are at once subtle and mysterious. They seem to speak of the earth's secrets and the forest's riches. Many have thought them aphrodisiacs; the smell will tell you why.

Truffles come both white and black, fresh and canned or frozen. They are always beastly expensive and, when at all possible, should be fresh.

The season for both white and black is late fall to early winter, which can take you through the holidays. As a cook and eater, I can think of no more lavish gift than a large black truffle in solitary splendor, or a white one nestled into Arborio rice. Since black truffles are often cooked, they are preserved by canning. White truffles, which are used raw, have recently been preserved by freezing.

The best black truffles came from France's Périgord, the best of white from Italy's Piedmont. The black truffles have a crinkled, leathery outer coating that needs to be pared away with the sharpest of small knives. Lightly cook the parings in a little white wine or broth; place in a small jar and seal tightly and refrigerate for future use in sauces. The white truffles do not need to be pared; but they need to be brushed—a soft toothbrush will do—to remove the dirt that lingers in the truffle's crevasses. The dirt protects the truffle until it is time to eat it. If you have trouble getting the dirt out, moisten the brush slightly. Try not to get the truffle wet. A true aficionado can tell you where the truffle comes from, and hence its quality, by the color of the clinging dirt. I am told that the finest have a very fine ocher dust.

Once the truffles have been cleaned, they should be used immediately. Just for yourself or a very dear friend, slice excellent French bread; spread it with good sweet butter; as thinly as possible—a truffle cutter will help—slice white truffles or finely chop black ones to make a coating for the butter; sprinkle with a little kosher salt and an imperceptible mist of freshly ground black pepper. Eat accompanied by a glass of your best red wine: heaven.

For more people or at another time, make a risotto using the rice in which a white truffle has been packed and adding more Arborio rice. Bring it to the table and there shave the white truffle on a truffle cutter—a sort of miniature coleslaw board in stainless steel—into a lavish topping for the risotto. This is rich and costly, so don't serve too much. A brilliantly colored or patterned earthenware plate will set off the pale color and the robust flavors.

The chopped black truffles can be cooked in butter and tossed with hot fresh noodles or cooked in a fine French pâté. Don't be as chintzy as the commercial pâté makers are. You need a lot of truffle to have its effects show up. Otherwise you are just wasting money.

Talk of truffles brings us neatly to foie gras and pâtés. Both are often cooked with black truffles tucked inside to perfume them. That is natural when the livers, specially fattened if from geese or ducks—don't ask how they get fat—come from the same region as the truffles. Now that livers come from Czechoslovakia, Israel and upstate New York, it is a less logical marriage. While you can buy canned cooked foie gras, I'm not much for it.

On the other hand, you can sometimes find whole livers gently cooked with their fat and sometimes Sauterne which is a perfectly happy flavor combination. All you need to do is slice them when cold. Try to acquire some brioche, the loaf kind, to slice, toast and serve alongside the pâté with a small knife and fork. If you are besotted with the idea of labor, you could make an aspic with Sauterne and white raisins that have been plumped up in the Sauterne. This is not necessary, but it is very pretty. The wine of sybaritic choice is Château d'Yquem. People think of sweet Sauterne as a dessert wine; but its full, lingering taste really does better not with the competition of a sweet, but with the rich, fatty complement of foie gras or a blue cheese (page 276). If Yquem is beyond reach, try Château Suduiraut, a sweety and fruity Moselle Beerenauslese, a California Gewürztraminer with a good hint of sugar, or a California late-harvest wine usually botrytisized—infected in such a way that much water is removed and both flavor and sweetness are intensified.

Standard pâtés, on the other hand, do better with rich, velvety red wines with some tannin. The tannin helps deal with the strong seasonings and pork flavors. The pâté's fats show off the wine and soften the tannin; it's altogether the perfect balance. Pâtés look well on yellow Luneville or blue and yellow Moustier pottery as well as American crafts people's earthenware like the strong brown and black glazed dishes of Marlboro Vermont's Malcolm Wright. The same kinds of dishes are attractive as platters if you put out the pâtés on a buffet or cut them in squares to spread on rounds of toast as hors d'oeuvre. Set off pâtés with crusty, peasanty breads, a selection of good mustards, cornichons or pickled onions, unless the pâtés are very upscale with hearts of foie gras, flecks of truffle, lashings of pistachio and succulences of sweetbreads. You will just have to use your good taste. By the way, if the price indicates that you are paying for truffles and foie gras, make sure that there is enough of both or either to justify the price. The foie gras is usually there to provide a contrast of texture. The truffles cannot do their job if they appear only as an occasional fleck of black.

If you are serving pâté for a party, the first move might be to check out the good stores in your area. They may make something succulent or sell one of the better nationally distributed brands. While many pâtés need a few days of aging to develop their full flavor, they should not be old unless properly frozen. This is the one luxury food I discuss that will probably be better when made nearer to your home.

The blue-veined cheeses such as Roquefort, Gorgonzola and, supremely, Stilton are yellowish and creamy with dots that may be as near green or gray as blue and are, historically, the class of the cheese world. My preference is generally for Stilton. In the United States, the Roquefort we get is unfortunately oversalted, due to import requirements. The Gorgonzola, while delicious, is a little easy and promiscuous, good as part of a cheese assortment or paired with a lemony salad. Stilton is the one to eat on its own instead of lunch, or as the perfect end of a meal. Stilton is crumbly in texture rather than spreadable; but it must not be dried out. It is meant to be eaten on dry, not sweet or salty, crackers or in chunks along with nuts. It is the Englishman's great cheese, a friend to wine, unlike Cheddar which seems a perfect beer cheese.

You can follow the French lead and serve a fine Sauterne; the flavor blend is perfect. I, however, follow English tradition, except that I will not leave the table to the men after the meal when I bring a whole or baby Stilton to the table wrapped in a large, clean white napkin. Along with it, I bring one of my collection of cheese scoops—of which more later—a bowl of nuts with a good nutcracker, a bowl of grapes in icewater with a grape shears (dreams of my own succession-houses at my country seat like an Edwardian gentleman), and above all a decanter of aged Port with heavy, small, cut-crystal Waterford Port glasses from which to sip. Plates, fruit knives and forks, nutpicks and English cheese crackers are all pleasant, but not essential.

When the Stilton gets to the table, I pick up

a sharp knife and cut a three- to four-inch-diameter circle through any coverings and through the rind of the cheese. Then I pick up a scoop, preferably one with a heavy, smooth ivory handle, and work the rounded silver bowl of the scoop through the cheese so as to bring out not a ball but a large sliver of cheese. As the cheese gets eaten, I keep scooping out the insides to form a hollow rind. This is what gets soused liberally with a lesser Port and then ground up into cheese spread. If the Stilton is more than a meal's worth, and I fondly hope so, I stuff the hollow with plastic wrap, and then wrap the entire cheese in more wrap and refrigerate. It needs to be taken from the refrigerator one hour before serving.

When selecting Port, remember, extravagant as a great Port may be, it has one redeeming feature: it doesn't spoil once opened as the equally costly Sauterne will. Simply put the stopper back in the decanter if you can stop drinking, and put the decanter in a dark place until you indulge again.

After such riches, dessert may seem excessive; but a little sweet luxury can sidle into the cheese and nut course and cause the evening to linger on until morning. Marrons glacés are a miracle the French play with the winter bounty of chestnuts. The chestnuts are swollen to almost twice their normal size in a sugar syrup. After the surface dries, they are dipped in a glazing sugar to become an incredibly suave and unctuous sweet. If you aren't having Port, sip a little of the Champagne left over from the caviar. A bottle of Roederer Cristal and a lavish box of marrons should be a gift to delight the most extravagant of high-living and rich-eating friends.

An American equivalent not one bit less good with its lineage in the desert is the medjool date. Its sweetness is produced by great fruit growing in the sun, then being dried to a plump and luscious state of preservation. These are expensive only when compared with other dates. They make a perfect and affordable gift. Make sure you are one of the recipients.

A NOTE ABOUT THE TYPE

This book was set in a typeface known as Bembo, which originated as a copy of a roman cut by Francesco Griffo for the Venetian printer Aldus Manutius. Deriving its name from its first use—in Cardinal Bembo's *De Aetna* in 1495—it was the forerunner of the standard European type for the next two centuries. In 1929 it was introduced by the English Monotype Corporation. The Bembo used in this book is a digitized adaptation of the Monotype face and was output on a Linotron 202 typesetter by Americomp, Brattleboro, Vermont.

This book was printed and bound by Arcata Graphics, Fairfield, Pennsylvania.